LATINO INVESTORS ENTREPRENEURS & ADVISORS

OFFICIAL 2021 GUIDE

ROBERT MILLER
HENRY PARK

FOREWORD BY
MR. ABC - AMADO HERNANDEZ

ISBN 978-0-9975887-9-8

NEWPORT COAST CLUB

LATINO INVESTORS ENTREPRENEURS & ADVISORS

OFFICIAL 2021 GUIDE

He who masters storytelling

rules the world.

A los eloteros, los paleteros,
los zapateros, los soñadores,
y todos los empresarios Latinos.

The only thing you've got in
this world is what you can sell.

— Arthur Miller
Death of a Salesman (1949)

LATINO INVESTORS ENTREPRENEURS & ADVISORS

OFFICIAL 2021 GUIDE

It is not true that people stop pursuing dreams because they grow old, they grow old because they stop pursuing dreams.

— Gabriel García Márquez

A NEW WAVE OF **LATINO** AND **LATINA** **INVESTORS,** **ENTREPRENEURS** AND **ADVISORS** IS EMERGING FROM THE PANDEMIC. **BADASS, STREET-SMART, AND TECH-SAVVY** – THEY ARE PASSIONATELY DRIVEN BEYOND SURVIVAL **TO CREATE TREMENDOUS WEALTH, PROTECT THE AMERICAN DREAM, SECURE THE FUTURE, AND EXPERIENCE AN AMAZING LIFESTYLE.**

The easiest way to make money is —
create something of such great value
that everybody wants to go out and
give and create value, the money
comes automatically.

— Jordan Belfort
The Wolf of Wall Street

May God continue to protect you and yours — remember the words of Joshua 1:9 — **Have I not commanded you? Be strong and courageous. Do not be afraid; do not be discouraged, for the Lord your God will be with you wherever you go.**

May God bless and keep you always
May your wishes all come true.
May you always do for others
And let others do for you
May you build a ladder to the stars
And climb on every rung
May you stay forever young
Forever young, forever young
May you stay forever young

— Forever Young — Bob Dylan
Bob Dylan (1973)

FOREWORD
MR. ABC — AMADO HERNANDEZ

Latinos can do anything.

— Roberto Aguire

Latinos do everything. We are dreamers and more. We are not afraid of hard work. We embrace challenges. We are innovators. We make an impact on society that is often silent — but is always positive and valuable.

Latino investor, entrepreneur and advisor pretty much describes my own professional career. So, when Robert Miller and Henry Park invited me to write the foreword for this book, I felt very qualified as well as honored.

This has been a difficult year for Latinos. Many of us have been disproportionately affected by the pandemic for one reason or another. But we are strong and naturally resilient. Belief in God, ourselves, and our Latino community will get us through these challenging times.

It was only a couple of months ago that I interviewed Robert and Henry on my show *Boost for the Day.* Robert and Henry had just published their first book together: *C19 Economics.* This is the third book that they have written together, and I am excited for you to read it.

Robert and Henry each have their own signature business styles and their styles, backgrounds and experience combine here in a unique, impactful, and powerful way.

FOREWORD — AMADO HERNANDEZ

2021 promises to be an amazing year for Latino investors, entrepreneurs, and advisors. After reading the pre-publication manuscript of this book I quickly realized why Robert and Henry subtitled it: *Official 2021 Guide.* This is an information packed and interactive resource for anyone doing business in the Americas.

From my own perspective as an investor, entrepreneur, and advisor, I expect to see increased activity in both commercial and global real estate well beyond 2021. This means great opportunities for Realtors®, lenders, and investors on both sides of the border.

I hope that you find this guide as valuable and inspiring as I did. I wish you success in whatever you road(s) you choose to travel.

Mr. ABC — Amado Hernandez

HE THAT WANTS TO BE THE GREATEST AMONGST YOU, LET HIM BE A SERVANT

Matthew 20:26

SEAMOS REALISTAS
Y HAGAMOS LO IMPOSIBLE.

— Che Guevara

PREFACE
ROBERT MILLER

When life itself seems lunatic, who knows where madness lies? Perhaps to be practical is madness. To surrender dreams — this may be madness. Too much sanity may be madness — and maddest of all: to see life as it is, and not as it should be.

— Miguel de Cervantes
Don Quixote

Waylon Jennings sings: "I've always been crazy but it's kept me from going insane." Maybe you must be a little crazy to be a Latino Investor, Entrepreneur or Advisor in this C19 Economy — but maybe it's the only way to keep from going insane!

PREFACE — ROBERT MILLER

There is a Spanish idiomatic expression — *comerse el coco* — which literally translates to "devour a coconut" but has a lot of other meanings.

Sometimes *comerse el coco* means "drive yourself crazy" by thinking about something so much that you just keep going around in circles and never really get anywhere.

In these *challenging times* (the term that has been literally over-exploited by corporate America along with *"we're all in this together"*) you might refer to the pandemic — and all its direct and collateral damage — by telling people *me estoy comiendo el coco* meaning "I've had it with thinking about the pandemic and it's driving me coconuts."

So, *me estoy comiendo el coco* and that's why I decided to write this book with my friend and partner Henry Park. This is my fourth book published during the pandemic and third authored with Henry — and we hope it will be our best.

PREFACE — ROBERT MILLER

Neither Miller nor Park are typical Latino surnames so you might be wondering why a gringo and a chino have written a book about Latino investors, entrepreneurs, and advisors. Hopefully by the end of this book you will realize the passion and commitment we have for the Latino community.

Let's stop *comiendo el coco* and emerge from this nightmare together — **BADASS, STREET-SMART and TECH SAVVY** — to create tremendous wealth, protect the American Dream, secure the future, and experience an amazing lifestyle. Let's keep in mind the words of JFK: "God's work must truly be our own.".

God Bless you and your loved ones. Stay safe — and remember to always wash your hands for lunch.

Robert Miller
Irvine, California
January 1, 2021

FOR NOTHING WILL BE IMPOSSIBLE WITH GOD.
Luke 1:37

In a way we are magicians. We are alchemists, sorcerers and wizards. We are a strange bunch. But there is great fun in being a wizard.

— Billy Joel

CONTENTS

If you want to find the secrets of the universe, think in terms of energy, frequency and vibration.

— Nikola Tesla

ONE
COURAGE TO DREAM

Deserve your dream.

— Octavio Paz

In 2021 we will be publishing a companion book — *Latinos: Courage to Dream* — a collection of personal stories about Latinos and Latinas. If you are interested in contributing your story, please send an email to: RobertMillerNow@Gmail.com.

Here is the story of Georgina Hernandez — a young influential Latina mother of two, wife, Real Estate Agent, and Author — who has the courage to dream and shares her pandemic experience. Please read her amazing story and reach out to her with yours.

GEORGINA HERNANDEZ

What Does an Influential Latina Do During Covid-19?

My name is Georgina Hernandez. I am a Latina woman, a mom of two daughters, a wife, a Real Estate Agent and an Author. I was born in Huntington Beach, California on April 14, 1983. My three brothers and I were raised by both my parents. My father and mother were born in Mexico and came to America in search of a better future for us. We moved to San Diego, California when I was 5 years old and I grew up in a small town called San Ysidro. We lived day by day while my father worked very hard to put food on the table and feed all 6 of us and my mom stayed home to raise us.

I loved growing up in San Ysidro! Ninety four percent of the population living there were Latinos so I learned to love my culture at a very young age. I grew up walking to Tijuana to visit my grandparent's and Spanish was my first language. I speak, read, and write in both English and Spanish fluently and I am very proud of being a

2

Mexican American. I love both my cultures as the warrior mentality of my Mexican side has kept me strong and motivated during this pandemic and my action taking American side has helped me take action to help and inspire others.

During this pandemic I have become a teacher to both my daughters, a chef, a housekeeper, a secretary to my husband who is working from home and so much more. It has been very challenging for all of us to be under one roof 24 hours a day 7 days a week but we have made it work and have been beyond blessed!

During these times many things have happened. Good things like spending time at home with the family to spending less money and saving more! but we have also seen a lot of negative things happen like the killing of George Floyd and the Riots that started towards the end of May. This was a very dark and scary time for me. It broke my heart but also gave me the courage to take action and finally do what had been tugging on my heart for a while.

I felt so much compassion over all those innocent lives being killed and mistreated and I feared for the future of our children and our nation. I just couldn't stay with these hopeless feelings so I had to be part of this movement for change.

This is when I decide to write my first Children's book titled *I Am Who I Say I Am*. The purpose of my book is to empower our children to love and celebrate who they are no matter what skin color they are! I know that I can't change the past, but I can positively impact the future of our children. So, with the help and inspiration of my two daughters, the guidance of my friend and mentor and my determination to be part of a better America, I started putting the book together and on August 15, 2020 I publish my book in English and Spanish that are available now on Amazon.com.

https://www.amazon.com/who-say-Georgina-Hernandez/dp/B08DST1X8Y/ref=sr_1_1?dchild=1&keywords=georgina+hernandez&qid=1598593734&sr=8-1

.

GEORGINA HERNANDEZ

This pandemic has truly been a blessing in disguise for my family and me. I am so happy that during this time of uncertainty and so much fear I have raised up to the opportunity of being a Latina leader and being part of this movement for change. I am honored to be able to share my story with all of you and to remind you that no matter where you come from, no matter what skin color you are or what language you speak, the dreams that are in your hearts are there for a reason and no one can take those away from you. No pandemic, no fear, no hate, no injustice, and no uncertainty will take away your light and your purpose in life. I want to encourage you to shine bright everywhere you go and awaken that Latino/a leader in you especially during these hard times.

"Life is tough but so are you" (Unknown)

Sincerely,

Georgina Hernandez
Realtor® DRE 02020287
Instagram/Facebook @georginafaithfamily
georginasellsre@gmail.com

5

The Latina in me is an ember
that blazes forever.

— Sonia Sotomayor

It is not true that people stop pursuing dreams because they grow old, they grow old because they stop pursuing dreams.

— Gabriel García Márquez

The biggest risk is not taking any risk… In a world that is changing really quickly the only strategy that is guaranteed to fail is not taking risks.

— Mark Zuckerberg

TWO
LA VIDA LOCA
ROBERT MILLER

In this country you gotta make the money first. Then when you get the money, you get the power. Then when you get the power, you get the women.

— Tony Montana (Al Pacino)
Scarface (1983)

Are you Latino — or wanna be? What's your perception of the Latino Community — from the inside or from the outside? Read on and you will discover the complexity, diversity, and attraction of Latinos.

The stereotypes of Latinos (aka "Hispanics") are many and very different. You may not remember "The Frito Bandito" — an animated character modeled after a stereotypical Mexican revolutionary in Frito-Lay commercials (1967-1971).

Fictional character Juan Valdez was created by Madison Avenue to promote the Federatión National de Cafeteros de Colombia (Fedecafé). Juan Valdez was portrayed on television ads by a Cuban actor.

Disney released *The Three Caballeros* in 1944. And then there was *Three Amigos* in 1986. In between we had dozens and dozens of Zorro shows on television and the big screen. We even had a gay Zorro in 1981 (*Zorro, The Gay Blade*).

We had Desi Arnaz, Xavier Cugat and Charo. There was a sitcom starring comedian Paul Rodriguez about a family in East Los Angeles with an abuela and a parrot. The most ridiculous was Bill Dana, an actor of Hungarian-Jewish ancestry, playing a dim-witted Bolivian astronaut repeating the words: "My name... José Jiménez."

Between Hollywood, Madison Avenue, and the Talking Heads on Big Media, it's almost impossible to define *Latino* and *Hispanic*.

If you think anything has changed, you're wrong. What do you think about these lines from *The Fix* (2017) by David Baldacci? "Two men climbed out, one large and one small. Pistols were in their waistbands. The large man was white — the small man — Hispanic."

So what are you supposed to envision about the "Hispanic" man? Do you think about Ricky Ricardo coming in the door and yelling "Lucy, I'm home!" Or does another Cuban come to mind — Tony Montana (Al Pacino) in *Scarface* (1983) holding a machine gun and screaming: wanna play rough? Okay! Say hello to my little friend!" So WTF is "Hispanic" supposed to mean? Someone like Cheech Marin or George Lopez — JLo or Selena?

So why does any of this even matter — or does it? *Latino Investors Entrepreneurs & Advisors* was written to help Latinos think differently and inspire them to create tremendous wealth, protect the American Dream, secure the future, and experience an amazing lifestyle.

If you consider yourself "Latino" — regardless of what you mark on your census form — it's critical that you understand the big picture, how you fit into it, and how you can color outside the lines to reshape as many pieces of the puzzle as possible.

Latinos, by choice, live "la vida loca" — but it's a different "loca" than college students crossing the border to do jello shots in a shithole bar. And it's a different "loca" than tourists doing Tequila shooters in some bougie nightclub on the "Mexican Riviera".

What, then, is livin' "la vida loca"? Maybe to a fault, Latinos live today for today. And they live it passionately. That doesn't mean that Latinos don't dream — Latinos are the world's biggest dreamers and they dream as passionately as they live.

The Latino World is big — it covers the entire globe from Alaska to Tierra del Fuego. Latinos come from all over the world and come in all colors. So what excites Latinos and how do you know if you are really Latino?

Do you start dancing when you hear Héctor Levoe (El Cantante) or Shakira singing "Hips Don't Lie"? How about Los Lobos singing "La Bamba"? Do you get emotional when you hear Jorge Negrete sing "Ay! Jalisco, no te rajes!"?

Do you know the story of Los Niños Héroes or the Battle of Boyacá — the Mexican-American War or the Spanish-American War?

In more current times, do you know about the Sleepy Lagoon murder in Los Angeles or about Salvador Agron, a poor and illiterate Puerto Rican immigrant from New York City's Upper West Side? Do you understand the "Latino Experience" from your own perspective and that of others?

13

If you are a "gringo" you must understand that there's more to the Latino community than Taco Tuesday and Cinco de Mayo — Mexican Beer and Tequila. Forget about "The Latino (or Hispanic) Market". Be aware that all Latinos are not Mexicans — but that all Mexicans are Latinos (if they choose to be).

And you must understand that, just because they're not painting mottos on streets and tearing down statues, Latinos have paid their dues when it comes to discrimination.

The pandemic has hit the Latino community disproportionately hard but many Latinos continue to work in unsafe conditions and dream of a better life.

This book is not about the *opportunity* to become super rich — it is about your *responsibility* to become as rich as you can so that you can make an enormous positive impact on the Latino Community. Like Tony Montana (*Scarface*) said: "… when you get the money, you get the power".

LA VIDA LOCA

Maybe there's a little **crazy** in all of us —
and maybe a little (or a lot) of **Latino** — you
have to have both for this book to have
maximum benefit for you.

If you take our book seriously — really
seriously — this book will change your life.
If you don't get it after reading this chapter
you might as well forget it.

The Latino Culture is amazingly rich. But,
more importantly, it is very spiritually
based. From Templo Mayor in Tenochlitlan
to the citadel of Machu Picchu to Laguna
Guatavita — the spirits of ancestors
(ancient and recent) continue to influence
is in all ways — in our food, traditions,
dance, song, and music.

But the real thing that binds Latinos
together is our belief in God and our belief
in ourselves and our families. *No importa
de donde sean — todos somos Latinos.*

Own your book —make notes, turn over
pages, highlight words and phrases, and fill
in the blanks. Live *la vida loca!*

Sometimes you're flush and sometimes you're bust, and when you're up it's never as good as it seems, and when you're down, you never think you'll be up again, but life goes on.

— George Jung (Johnny Depp)
Blow (2001)

The idea is not
to live forever,
but to create
*something
that will.*

— ANDY WARHOL

THREE
ANYONE CAN COOK
HENRY PARK

In the past, I have made no secret of my distain for Chef Gasteau's famous motto: "Anyone can cook." But I realize, only now do I truly understand what he meant. Not everyone can become a great artist, but a great artist can come from anywhere.

— Anton Ego (Peter O'Toole)
Ratatouille (2007)

Not everyone can become a millionaire, but a millionaire can come from anywhere.

was twelve years old when lightning struck me. I was a Korean kid, born in Guan, living in the barrio. On a beautiful sunny Southern California sunny afternoon, I rode my bike down the San Gabriel river channel from Hawaiian Gardens to Huntington Beach.

I dreamed of escaping the *hood* and living with the "rich" people at the beach. More precisely, I wanted to live in one of those big houses looking out at the Pacific Ocean.

So, on Saturdays I rode my bike to the ocean and did some serious "California Dreaming." After a long ride I arrived at the beach this particular Saturday and began cruising around and looking at houses. And there it was — the house of my dreams. Wow. And it was for sale!

As I walked in to the "Open House" to grab a flyer from the rack on the counter I was stopped by an older man who asked me what I wanted. I told him I wanted a flyer and asked him the price of the house.

ANYONE CAN COOK — HENRY PARK

He looked down at me in the most dismissive and demeaning way and one that I have never forgotten and replied: "More than you could ever afford, buddy."

Thirteen years later I bought the house next door for $420,000 with a down payment of almost 50%. What happened to me in after the old guy blew me away?

You're going to have to read this book — or skip to *Keeping Up with Henry* at the back. But I will tell you that somewhere along the way I realized that being poor has no color lines. The Latinos I grew up with thought that I was a rich Asian kid who didn't know what it was like to be poor.

And so, I had a chip on my shoulder — the older I got the more resentful I became. I got fire in my belly to make money. And I made it my life's mission to be successful.

Like Chef Gasteau's motto says: "Anyone can cook". And that includes YOU. Join me on Henry Park's Road to A Million. Be relentless. Be ferocious. Dare to be rich!

Make your
life's mission
to be
successful.

F O U R
TAKE CONTROL

With a good conscience our only sure reward, with history the final judge of our deeds, let us go forth to lead the land we love, asking His blessing and His help, but knowing that here on earth God's work must truly be our own.

— John F, Kennedy
Inaugural Address (1961)

**EXPLORE
DISCOVER
CREATE
INSPIRE**

God's work must truly be our own. Those were the final words of John F, Kennedy's Inaugural Address delivered on a bitterly cold January 20th in Washington, D.C. almost sixty years ago. The 40 mph winds were so loud that even those on the platform with him could not hear his historic speech. But the words remain true today — and will remain forever true.

To create tremendous wealth, protect the American Dream, secure the future, and create an amazing lifestyle you need to take control of your life now. Believing in God is great, but you must believe in yourself. And you must take immediate steps to **TAKE CONTROL** of your life.

This book was written to help you take control of your life so that you can realize all of your dreams. It's not an impossible thing to do. You don't need a "Life Coach" or "Business Coach". You don't need to attend a weeklong "boot camp" to prove you're badass. Everything you need is in your heart and mind —and in this book.

TAKE CONTROL

There are four things that you should be doing every day of your life — **EXPLORE** — **DISCOVER** — **CREATE** — **INSPIRE**. The same four things — everyday.

But before you jump into this cycle you need to do a few things to prepare yourself for success. Before you plant your garden, you must remove the weeds and rocks. You must eliminate all obstacles that you can — and that includes both people and things. But, most important, you must eliminate your own negative thoughts.

Reach deep into your soul and find the courage and wisdom to take control of your future right now. Maybe the answer comes from God — or maybe from some other source. Wherever you might find it take immediate action and assume responsibility for creating tremendous wealth, securing your future, and experiencing an amazing lifestyle.

Do everything in your power to save the American Dream for yourself and your family. Take control and dare to be great.

TAKE CONTROL

How are you going to take control NOW?

_____

_____

_____

_____

_____

_____

_____

_____

_____

_____

_____

_____

_____

_____

_____

_____

_____

_____

RAINMAKING

When it comes to rainmaking, there's clearly a reason why God gave us two ears but only one mouth.

— Guy Kawasaki

Rainmaking is impacting the world through the power of emotions and the magic of storytelling. Check out *"Rainmaking"* on Amazon.com.

RAINMAKING

How are you going to make it rain?

EXPLORE

It is a big and beautiful world. Most of us live and die in the same corner where we were born, and never get to see any of it. I don't want to be most of us.

— Oberyn Martell
Game of Thrones

Explore the world without ever leaving home.

EXPLORE

What do you think about Walter Mitty?

DISCOVER

Only when the tide goes out do you discover who's been been swimming naked.

— Warren Buffett

Discover the world. Discover every moment of your life. Look under every rock. Ask questions. Become a human telescope and a human microscope.

DISCOVER

Can you stay off the grid long enough to discover a "brave new world"?

_____

_____

_____

_____

_____

_____

_____

_____

_____

_____

_____

_____

_____

_____

_____

_____

_____

_____

_____

CREATE

The best way to predict the future is to create it.

— Abraham Lincoln

Create your future every single nanosecond that you are alive. Like James Dean said: "Dream as if you'll live forever. Live as if you'll die today."

CREATE

What have you created (or will create) that will live forever?

INSPIRE

The most important thing is to try and inspire people so that they can be great in whatever they want to do.

— Kobe Bryant

When Steve Jobs was trying to get John Scully to leave Pepsi and join Apple he asked: "Do you want to sell sugar water the rest of your life or come with me and change the world?"

INSPIRE

What inspires you?

TAKE CONTROL

This is not a textbook. It is a highly personalized guide designed to help you create great wealth and income as an entrepreneur. The reason we mention this again is that succeeding in business is not as easy as it sounds. But this guide can help make it easier.

Here is how you are going to maximize your ROI on the cost of this book and the time will invest reading it and making your notes and plans. Skim through the remaining pages of this book to get an idea of the material that is presented in each of the chapters.

Beginning with this first chapter keep track of how much time it takes you to read the chapter and make your notes.

Once you know how long it takes for you to complete a chapter make a schedule for completing your entire book. Dedicate the time required to ensure that you devote enough time to master the concepts that we are providing to you. Mastering the concepts in this book is a self-investment.

IT IS OUR CHOICES THAT SHOW WHAT WE TRULY ARE, FAR MORE THAN OUR ABILITIES.

— J.K. Rowling

FIVE
DREAMS

Reality is wrong. Dreams are for real.

— Tupak Shakur

Our greatest challenge is not ending the pandemic or restoring law and order — it is saving the American Dream.

DREAMS

What are your dreams — do you dream of great wealth? If so, this book is for you. This book is for dreamers. This book is for everyone who wants to make a lot of money by working smart — not by working hard.

The American Dream has changed greatly over the past four hundred years and will continue to evolve. The American Dream was once based on the "work ethic" — the belief that hard work, discipline, and frugality would someday be rewarded by something. That "something" usually meant being to "retire comfortably."

What is wrong with that picture? Think about it. You start working at fifteen and work "hard" for fifty years. Then you can retire and "enjoy" your life. Help us with the math. Let's say that you expect to live until eighty. Eighty minus sixty-five is fifteen. So, you enjoy the first fifteen years of your life. You then work fifty years to enjoy maybe fifteen years. How well you take care of yourself will determine how much you will enjoy your final years.

DREAMS

The American Dream started unwinding when many discovered that there was no pot of gold at the end of the rainbow after working hard their whole lives. In 1949 Arthur Miller wrote a play titled *Death of a Salesman* about a salesman named Willie Loman. Willie Loman felt humiliated by his failure and committed suicide. The death of a salesman became the death of a dream for poor Willie.

Latinos have always believed in the American Dream — and that may be a big problem because our American Dream is being threatened more than any time in our lives. These days American Dream is being threatened from both outside America — and from within. A major blow came when China intentionally released its deadly virus causing a global pandemic forcing the world to shut down. The economic and emotional costs are immeasurable.

Millions of businesses have closed, and millions of businesses will never reopen. The pandemic has quickly turned thriving businesses into zombies struggling and other businesses have been able to pivot and innovate ways to survive. Failure has become a constant reality. It is getting harder to keep our dreams alive.

Before the pandemic Latino prosperity was on a historic roll as Latinos road the wave of America's longest expansion ever. A record number of Latino families were buying homes, wages were rising, and unemployment was down. Even though the outlook for Latinos was looking good, Latino wealth and income greatly lagged non-Latino white wealth and income.

The pandemic has hit our community disproportionately hard and the prosperity gap is continuing to widen significantly. We do not need to explain the reasons that this is happening or how serious it is. If you are Latino, you are experiencing it — if you are not it does not matter.

Latino Investors Entrepreneurs & Advisors was written to help you save your dreams, restore lost dreams, and create new ones. This is not a collection of studies made by professors or "Latino" experts. It is a book for Latino entrepreneurs written by entrepreneurs. Our book is intentionally simple — written in sixth-grade English.

This book may be the wackiest book you have ever read. It is intended to be fun and direct — and to provide you with immediate strategies to grow your business.

The main objective of this book is to help you create great income and wealth and enjoy the lifestyle of your dreams. We believe the quickest and easiest way for you to create great income and wealth is for you to work for yourself — you will never get rich working for someone else. And without prosperity you will never achieve the American Dream.

For most Latinos, the American Dream has several components that all have a lot do with the value of the Latino family and community. Home ownership and college education is are a big part of the dream along with owning a business.

With income and wealth usually lower than the average for some Latino families, home ownership and college education may seem like dreams that may never come true.

Wealth is usually created in one of two ways — real estate investment or business ownership. And business ownership can focus can involve real estate). There are many roads to entrepreneurship including growing an existing business, starting an business, and buying one.

Latinos have made a lot of money in the real estate industry as professionals but the real wealth has been made by Latinos who have had the courage and talent to invest in real estate. Many have started with very little and have built substantial property portfolios — one property at a time —investing in single family or multi-unit residential properties.

Business ownership can range from selling peanuts, flowers, or oranges at the freeway exits to major retail or manufacturing firms. The possibilities are unlimited.

DREAMS

What are your dreams?

COURAGE IS BEING
SCARED TO DEATH, BUT
SADDLING UP ANYWAY.

— JOHN WAYNE

SIX
LATINOS

In the end, the American dream is not a sprint or even a marathon, but a relay. Our families do not always cross the finish line in the span of one generation. But each generation passes on to the next the fruits of their labor.

— Julian Castro

The Latino community in America controls tremendous wealth and will continue to grow exponentially. You do not have to be Latino or speak Spanish to participate in the Latino Wealth Experience, but you must understand Latino values and be passionate about helping.

LATINOS

America is on the edge. It is late September and our lives have been turned upside down since China intentionally released their deadly virus on the world at the beginning of this year. Many of us feel like Paul Simon in his song *American Tune*:

And I don't know a soul who's not been battered
I don't have a friend who feels at ease
I don't know a dream that's not been shattered
or driven to its knees
But its all right, it's all right
We've lived so well so long
Still when I think of the road
we're traveling on
I wonder what went wrong
I can't help it, I wonder what went wrong

What went wrong? Somehow, we went from *living the dream* to *Helter Skelter.* It's not only the American Dream that is being threatened — it's our economy and our American way of life. We are weeks away from what is being described as "the most important election of our lives." Latinos have emerged as a bigger factor than anyone could have ever imagined.

LATINOS

Who are "Latinos"? First, Latinos are not Hispanics. Although many people and companies use the terms "Latino" and "Hispanic" interchangeable — they are not.

The term "Hispanic" was adopted by the administration of Richard Nixon. In 1980 the Census Bureau first used "Hispanic" on its forms. Since then many people have allowed themselves to be labeled as "Hispanic" without realizing that they were being exploited.

Political leaders, companies, and the press do not know which term to use. In the 2016 presidential election both Hillary Clinton and Donald Trump used both "Hispanic" and "Latino" to mean the same thing — often in the same sentence.

Company advertising uses both terms, and the press is worse — using both "Hispanic" and "Latino" interchangeably in opposition to the term "white." To many the word "Hispanic" has negative connotations — and some believe that the word "Hispanic" has racial overtones.

Dictionary definitions of the word Hispanic are conflicting and confusing. For example, *Dictionary.com* offers two noun definitions: "a citizen or resident of the United States who is of Spanish or Spanish-speaking Latin American descent" and "a person whose *Merriam-Webster.com* presents two adjective definitions: "of, or relating to, or being a person of Latin American descent and especially of Cuban, Mexican, or Puerto Rican origin living in the United States" and "of or relating to the people, speech, or culture of Spain".

What's wrong with labeling "Hispanics" based on geography and or language? Brazil is the largest country in South America and was founded by Portugal — and the official language of Brazil is Portuguese.

The biggest issue with the term "Hispanic" is that most of the people allow themselves to be labeled as "Hispanics" have no idea what the term means — or was intended to mean when the government created it. They allow themselves to be marginalized.

LATINOS

We prefer "Latino" to "Hispanic" because the word "Hispanic" glorifies the Spanish Empire that colonized most of Latin America. The Spaniards — along with the Portuguese —exploited and enslaved native Americans and brought slaves from Africa to Latin America.

Latino is short for "Latinoamericano" (Latin American). But it is not that simple these days. There are so many Hispanic labels engrained in government agencies, corporate advertising and initiatives, and trade associations and other organizations.

Latino — NOT Latinx — is a better choice. But we are not born Latino — we proudly choose to be Latino. We choose to embrace the Latino lifestyle, culture, food, drink, music, dance, and values of Nuestra Comunidad Latina.

You may wonder why so much attention has been given to the "Latino vs. Hispanic" issue. Latino is more than ancestry — it is a lifestyle you must embrace to be an Latino entrepreneur who serves our community.

LATINOS

The back pages of the Latino culture are filled with badass heroes from los Niños Héroes de Chapultepec — to Cesar Chavez. There are too many to list here, but you should watch the six hour PBS documentary *Latino Americans.*

Latino Americans features 500 years of history and 100 interviews with Latinos. You will learn that there are 4,000 years of badass Latinos. And you will probably be surprised to discover amazing stories of unsung heroes.

Most of us were taught that the great heroes were Christopher Columbus and Hernán Córtez — that could not be farther from the truth. Invest the time. And Montezuma may not be the badass you believe him to be.

To be a successful badass entrepreneur or advisor you must understand what went down in Latin America in the last 30,000 years — and especially in the last 500 years. Watch *John Leguizamo's Latin History for Latins.* Beyond funny it is right on — it is a real revelation.

LATINOS

Do you have a real Latino or Latina hero? What about investing an hour each week and learn about Simón Bolívar or Fernando Botero — or Gabriel García Márquez or Eva Perón.

Mandatory reading for every Latino — or those who want to be Latino — should be Victor Villaseñor's *Rain of Gold*. *Rain of Gold* is the story of the author's three generations of overcoming poverty, prejudice, and economic exploitation.

The Latinoamericano experience is one of the richest in the history of the world. The empires of the Aztec, Maya, and Inca civilizations are the most known but there are many other wonderful stories.

These days — especially these days — America is focused on Black Lives Matter. History — real history — reveals that Latinos have survived centuries of genocide and systematic racism.

Native Americans — from all the Americas — have endured discrimination and exploitation since the first "foreigners" stepped off ships from Europe or flying saucers from outer space.

Those stories we were taught about the Spanish arriving in California and helping the "savages" by converting them Christianity are now disgusting. There were hints of the brutality and exploitation in the old *Zorro* movies — but they were veiled hints.

Were the heroes we grew up watching in Disney movies really heroes? You know the ones — Davy Crockett and Jim Bowie. And Andrew Jackson — the "Indian Killer." The heroes were really villains.

Fuggedabout what happened hundreds of years ago. Let us look at the last hundred years. Mexico, for example, has been repeatedly used as a temp agency for labor. When we need workers we invite them here and pick them up at the border. When we do not need them anymore, we round them up and ship them back. Where is the fairness in that?

When the Great Depression hit, and jobs disappeared hundreds of thousands (if not millions) of Mexicans and Mexican Americans were deported to Mexico. Some people estimate that half of them were birthright citizens of the United States.

The United States did the same thing when we needed workers during World War II. With America's men and women fighting the war there was a shortage of workers in the factories and fields. So, again, we welcomed workers from Mexico with open arms. In fact, we advertised for them. When the war ended, and we did not need them anymore we shipped them back just like we did in the 1930's.

Why is it important to know all of this? It is important to know that what Latinos have been through — how they have been mistreated and how they have responded to that mistreatment. Many people attribute "Living well is the best revenge." as being an old Spanish proverb. It was really a quote from George Herbert — a 16th century poet but it is better in Spanish.

Sin embargo, dicen que vivir bien es la major venganza. And that's exactly what Latinos must continue to do — we must continue living well.

The best way for us to live well is as successful Latino **innovators**, **investors**, **entrepreneurs**, and **advisors**.

This book was written to inspire you and help you create tremendous wealth, protect the American Dream, secure the future, and create an amazing lifestyle.

The most important thing — and the first step — is for you to think about **why** you want to be a Latino entrepreneur or advisor.

For as long as I can remember everyone has wanted a piece of the "Hispanic market." Hispanic! Hispanic! Hispanic! Ad nauseum. How long has there been a "Hispanic Foods" section in your supermarket? How much does Madison Avenue spend each year chasing Latinos? Do they really understand our community?

Experts estimate that the economic outlook of over 60 million Latinos in America represent over $2 trillion (with a T), and that U.S. Latino GDP equates to the 7th or 8th largest economy in the world.

What role are you going to play in the future of Latinos in America? How passionate are you about our culture? Our culture represents the heritage of countries from the tip of South America to the U.S. Mexican border. And it includes countries in the Caribbean and U.S. territory Puerto Rico.

The Spanish may have destroyed American empires with colonization and genocide. They may have stolen and melted down priceless pre-Columbian treasures. But the *corazón, alma y vida* lives in the Latino people and always will.

Fernando Botero painted his "fat people." Vicente Fernandez beautifully is "El Rey de la Música Ranchera. What impact are you going to make as a Badass Latino? El futuro es tuyo.

LATINOS

You are not born "Latino" — it's a choice that you consciously make. "Latino" is not a race, nationality, or ethnicity. Federal policy defines "Hispanic" as not a race , but an ethnicity. Latinos and Latinas come in all sizes, shapes, and colors. They come from all countries. And they may, or may not, speak Spanish.

What, then, makes a Latino or Latina a Latino or Latina? Passion for life.
Love of family. All kinds of music — and all the dancing and singing that comes with it. The Latino culture is hands-down the most diversified, exciting, richest culture that has ever existed.

To be successful as a Latino Investor, Entrepreneur, and/or Advisor you must sincerely embrace the culture. Forget about all those "Hispanic Marketing" seminars and consultants. Forget about the merely capitalizing on the "Latino Market". Unless you are ready, willing, and able to become a n integral part of the Latino Community you will never succeed. The view is so much different from the outside.

58

LATINOS

What is your definition of "Latino"?

Porfirio Diaz • Eva Perón • Los Niños Héroes de Chapultepec • **Fidel Castro** • Simón Bolívar • **Ricky Martin** • Luis Fonzi • **Emiliano Zapata** • Pancho Villa • **Jennifer Lopez** • Edward James Olmos • **Vicente Fernandez** • Leslie Grace • **Romeo Santos** • Selena • Salma Hayak • Cantinflas • Jorge Negrete • Dolores del Río • **Diego Rivera** • **Shakira** • **Ritchie Valens** • Celia Cruz • **Tito Puente** • Carlos Santana • Che Guevara • **Joan Baez** • Pitbull • **Daddy Yankee** • Menudo • Héctor Levoe • **Carlos Vives** • Prince Royce • **Fernando Botero** • Willie Colón • Eva Longoria • **Ricardo Montalbán** • **John Leguizamo** • Victor Villaseñor • **Sofia Vergara** • Maná • Xavier Cugat • Charo • **Desi Arnaz** • Rita Moreno • **Gloria Estefan** • Gabriel García Márquez • **Cheech Marin** • **You**

SEVEN
LATIN AMERICA

To our sister republics south of our border, we offer a special pledge — to convert our good words into good deeds — in a new alliance for progress — to assist free men and free governments in casting off the chains of poverty.

— John F. Kennedy
Inaugural Address (1961)

What's the difference between a "Latino" and a "Latin American"?

Latin America is the most amazing and exciting place in the world. From the tip of Patagonia to the Mexico-U.S. border are the many countries that make up Latin America. Definitions of Latin America vary somewhat but here we are including:

Puerto Rico
Mexico
Guatemala
Honduras
El Salvador
Nicaragua
Costa Rica
Panama
Colombia
Venezuela
Ecuador
Peru
Bolivia
Chile
Argentina
French Guiana
Paraguay
Uruguay
Brazil
Cuba
Dominican Republic

LATIN AMERICA

We define **Latin America** as the parts of the Americas that were once colonies of Spain (New Spain), Portugal (Colonial Brazil), or France (New France) That definition could be expanded to include the parts of the Western United States that were once colonies of Spain, the land acquired by the Louisiana Purchase, and the French part of Canada (Quebec). Excluded are those places that were colonized by Great Britain. By that broader definition, the term "Latin American" is more accurate than the improperly used term "Latino". And it's important to note that "Latin America" does not include everything "south of the border".

For those of us who speak Spanish (Spanglish will not cut it) and may have friends, relatives, business associates, or contacts south of the border the future is bright — very bright.

Mexico and Colombia are top picks are will lead the pack in Latin America this decade. Mexico's economy is the second largest economy in Latin America, 15th largest in the world, and 11th in purchasing power. **Mexico** will continue to rebound from the pandemic hit and we expect a slowdown in inflation and lower interest rates over the coming months. We expect Mexico to steadily climb toward its 1980 rank of 10th largest economy in the world. There are enormous real estate opportunities in Mexico and increasing real estate transactions between Mexican and U.S. citizens and companies. Look for major investment in U.S. commercial real estate by Mexican individual and institutional investors.

Colombia is the fourth largest economy in Latin America and offers the highest ROI as its economic boom continues to roar. The opportunities in Colombia are virtually unlimited and warrant a fresh look.

Finally let's not forget about **Puerto Rico**. Puerto Rico, a Caribbean island, has been a U.S. territory since the United States defeated Spain in the Spanish-American War. The economy of Puerto Rico is the most competitive in Latin America.

Latin American countries I have visited (or will visit in 2021).

Yes. Latinos dream more.
When you live in poverty, when
your president is imposed upon
you, when they kill someone and
no one gets indicted, and when
only a few get rich, of course you
dream more. It's no coincidence
that magic realism happens in
Latin America, because for us
dreams and aspirations are part
of life.

—Jorge Ramos

EIGHT
BUSINESS

After all, the chief business of the American people is business. They are profoundly concerned with producing, buying, selling, investing and prospering in the world. I am strongly of the opinion that the great majority of people will always find these the moving impulses of our life.

— Calvin Coolidge

Be sure you are not just creating a "job" for yourself, friends, and family.

BUSINESS

Business ownership offers you the most potential for creating great wealth. In addition to making money owning a business has other advantages. But it is not as easy as it sounds. It can be a road to heaven or to hell depending on you.

If you are already a business owner, you may be facing great challenges or have access to tremendous opportunities — depending on how you look at it. Many great fortunes are made in the worst of times. This is when you need to evaluate every aspect of your business, make a plan which is both realistic and agile, and take immediate steps not only to survive but to prosper during and after the pandemic.

If you do not own a business, there are several options open to you. You can choose to be a passive investor in a business or active investor. The difference is how much you will be involved in the management and operations of the business. You can choose to invest in a successful business or a turnaround situation — or decide to start a business.

BUSINESS

Whether you dream of pushing a paleta cart down Main Street or having the fanciest Mexican restaurant in New York every business starts with a dream. Nobody has ever expressed that better than Walt Disney when he said: "I hope we never lose sight of one thing — that it was all started by a mouse.

If you want to be an entrepreneur, you need to start with a dream. Billionaire Sir Richard Branson offers this advice: "My advice to aspiring entrepreneurs thinking of starting their own business is start small but always think big."

The following story has been told many times and its always a fisherman — often a Mexican fisherman. Our version of the story is about a Cuban fisherman from Havana. But the fisherman could be anywhere and at any time in history.

Jose was a third-generation fisherman who left Havana alone in his little boat to catch some fish. He needed to catch a dozen fish each day seven days a week because he would take the two best and biggest fish home to his wife to feed his family. He would sell the ten remaining fish to get the money he needed to live.

Each day when he left the pier his sights were set on catching his dozen fish as soon as possible. As soon as he caught twelve fish he was done for the day. Then he could sell ten fish at the dock, take two fish home to his wife along with most of the money he got from selling the others — saving a few pesos for a few glasses of rum and a cigar.

After dinner Jose would walk into town with his guitar to spend a few hours at his favorite bar. Once there he would tell fish stories with his friends, play guitar, drink, sing, and smoke a cigar before returning home.

Some days were not as good as others and Jose would stay out until dark trying to catch his dozen fish. On good days he would head back early and take a siesta before dinner. Why catch more fish?

BUSINESS

One day an American gangster was on the docks when Jose returned with his catch of the day. It was early afternoon with plenty of daylight left. The gangster admired the catch and asked Jose why he was back so early. Jose responded that he caught enough fish and wanted to take a nap before dinner; and that after dinner he would go to the paladar and drink rum with his friends, play guitar, and sing.

The gangster started lecturing Jose about being lazy and explained that — if he worked a little harder — he could someday have his own paladar. Jose laughed a little and asked how long that would take. The gangster replied, "not long, maybe 10 – 15 years." Jose thought a little and then replied: "and what would I do then?"

The gangster smiled and explained that Jose could retire. "Retire!" exclaimed Jose. "And then what would I do?" he asked the gangster. The gangster replied: "Whatever you want. Go fishing, nap in the afternoons, drink rum, play guitar and sing with your friends…" Jose thought about it and then responded to the gangster: "Gracias señor." And then Jose unloaded his catch and thought about his nap, dinner, and evening at the paladar. The gangster lit up a cigar and walked away thinking to himself "que perezoso".

Business is not for everyone — and it's hard to predict who will succeed and who will fail.

Before the pandemic there were probably over 70,000 "Mexican" restaurants operating in the United States — representing about 10% of the national restaurant landscape. How many of those Mexican restaurants were operating profitably? And how many of them are still in business?

Operating a Mexican restaurant, Cuban restaurant, Argentinian restaurant — any restaurant sounds sexier than it is. It is a lot of hard work and takes a really special type of person to deal with the endless hours and ongoing stress. But, done right, it can be an unbelievable experience.

BUSINESS

The first question you must ask yourself before starting or buying a business is "why?" If you currently own a business, you should ask yourself the same question. Remember that it's your **why**. This is the most difficult question to answer. And the answer must be more than just "to make lots of money".

Make sure that you are honest with yourself and that you understand all of the risks (in addition to the rewards) involved with owning and operating a business.

You probably already have an idea of **what** business you want to have. Conduct your due diligence and invest the time and energy to define exactly what kind of business and how big you want it to be.

Next is determining **where** your business will be located. Maybe it will be a virtual business or operate out of a "workspace." The pandemic has changed how we look at brick-and-mortar businesses. Remember "location, location, location" if you really even need a "location" — and think global.

When are you going to take action? Manaña? Once you have made a decision take immediate action.

How is going to require some time, maybe some money, and definitely some professional help. Don't try to second-guess your *how* because it is critical that you have a solid **Business Plan Outline** and **Business Plan Summary**.

Before you start on your Business Plan Outline and Business Plan Summary review the **TOOLBOX** at the end of your guide and familiarize yourself with the your tools: **60 Second Speech — Personal Plan — Game Plan — Playbook — Pitchdeck — Videos**.

Whether you have been in business most of your life or are just planning to get started in business, seriously consider investing in some professional help from an experienced and talented business advisor who can save you time and money. The right advisor could make the difference between your success and failure.

SAVING YOUR BUSINESS

D o you own a **ZOMBIE** business — a business that is on the verge of shutting down? Have you depleted your reserves? What are you going to do? Are you being realistic about saving your business? ¿Vale la pena?

If your business is struggling, you must take **immediate** action. The first thing to do is to seek help from a trusted advisor who can provide an accurate and objective analysis of your situation.

To some degree you are emotionally involved with your business. Your feelings can prevent you from making the best decision. An experienced business advisor can help you decide whether to do everything possible to attempt to save your business, try to sell it, or shut it down.

The worst thing you can do is to do nothing. If you do nothing you will simply be a **zombie company**

75

GROWING YOUR BUSINESS

Are you a business owner who is managing to survive the pandemic but want to grow your business? Forget about taking your business to "the next level" — take it to the moon! How are you going to do that?

This is an exceptionally exciting time to grow your business —the possibilities are unlimited.

There are two ways to grow your busines. First, you can try to do it yourself — without any help. Before you do that, you should ask yourself why you haven't already done so.

Second, get some professional help from an advisor with a track record — someone who has personally grown more than one business. Or someone who has helped others grow their businesses. But beware of a consultant or advisor who has nothing more to offer than **empty promises**

STARTING A BUSINESS

S tarting a business is very easy — starting one that is quickly profitable is not. Think long and hard about starting your own busines to make sure that your dream does not immediately turn into a nightmare.

To do it right you need the help of several advisors. You need a tax advisor to help you decide on the type of business entity (LLC/S-Corp./C-Corp.) and a business attorney to form your new business for you and help you with the necessary licenses, registrations, and permits.

Most important you need a team of badass business advisors to help you plan, launch, promote, and operate your business. Trying to do everything yourself is a certain **formula for failure**.

So where do you find the right advisors? We can help you. Our contact information is at the back of this book.

77

BUYING A BUSINESS

B uying a business without professional help can turn out to be a bigger disaster than starting one.

Buying a busines is a lot like buying a stock used car, or previously-owned real estate. Someone is selling it for a reason (or many reasons) and you have to be dead sure about **why** you are buying it.

Again, this is where you need professional help. For buying (or selling) small businesses you may want to consider engaging the services of a licensed **Business Broker**.

For medium and large businesses you will *definitely* need a qualified **Acquisition Team** which should include an **Investment Banker**, **Business Attorney**, and possibly an **Appraiser** or **Business Valuation Expert**. We can connect you with some of the best and the brightest people to help you have a great experience.

BUSINESS NOTES

Why I want to own a business.

BUSINESS NOTES

What business I want to own.

BUSINESS

Where my business will be located.

BUSINESS

When I will start or buy my business.

BUSINESS

How I am going to make my business super successful?

My Business Plan Outline

My Business Plan Summary

Carlos Slim
Mexico
Icon of success in Latin America.

Joseph Safra
Brazil
Founded Banco Safra while a teenager.

Dulce Pugliese de Godoy
Brazil
Co-founder of healthcare company.

Germán Larrea
Mexico
Mysterious banker and entrepreneur.

Luis Carlos Sarmiento
Colombia
Legendary banking guru.

NINE
INVESTORS

Appearances are much less important than the courage, discipline, and resolve of people who are economically productive.

— Thomas J. Stanley
The Millionaire Next Door

**For more information on investing join
"Henry Park's Road to a Million"
group on Facebook and or visit
"HenryParksRoadtoaMillion.com and order a
copy of Henry's new book
Henry Park's Road to a Million
On Amazon**

Investment by Latinos and Latinas is going to ramp-up to all-time highs in 2021. Here's why and how and where.

U.S. Latinos and Latin American investors are going to be major players in U.S. and global **commercial real estate** in the years to come. The major economic fallout from the pandemic will hit U.S. commercial real estate in Q1 2021 and a global wave will follow.

The commercial game has already begun to change with closed businesses, broken leases, and a flight to smaller or virtual workplaces.

With U.S. equity markets overbought savvy investors will turn to commercial real estate for safety, diversification, and income. Look for major Latin American institutional players to invest heavily — especially in Latino-dominated locations.

Private investors will heavily participate U.S. and global commercial real estate investing. There are going to be tremendous buys out there for investors with cash and credit.

The three principal arenas for creating great wealth in 2021 and beyond are the **Stock Market**, **Real Estate**, and **Business Ownership**. Let's take a look at these one at a time.

First, the **stock market**. We expect the Dow to jump from 30,000 to over 40,000 in the next four years. That is although the market is overbought. Equities are being propelled by a FOMO (Fear Of Missing Out) mentality — the emotion of pure unadulterated greed. And that greed will continue to push stocks upward.

Second, **real estate**. With real estate think **Commercial** and **Global**. Focus on quality properties in what may now be less-than-desirable locations. Think! Look for value and **leverage**.

Third, **business ownership**. The right business adequately capitalized and aggressively managed offers a much higher potential return-on-investment than both because it requires relatively more initial capital and a lot of time.

My Asset Allocation

My Investment Strategy

With a good perspective
on history, we can have a
better understanding of the
past and present, and thus a
clear vision of the future.

— Carlos Slim Helu

TEN
ENTREPRENEURS

Here's to the crazy ones. The misfits. The rebels. The troublemakers. The round pegs in the square holes. Those who see things differently. They're not fond of rules. And they have no respect for the status quo. You can quote them, disagree with them, glorify or vilify them. About the only thing you can't do is ignore them. Because they change things. They push the human race forward. And while some may see them as the crazy ones, we see genius. Because the people who are crazy enough to think they can change the world are the ones who do.

—Steve Jobs

Are you a crazy one? Misfit? Rebel? Troublemaker?

Entrepreneurs will combine the vision of **innovators** with the capital of **investors** and their own passion to make the American economy great again in spite of China's brazen attack and the efforts of internal agitators to create mass hysteria and paralyze our economy and society. There are two distinct types of entrepreneurs:

Small Businesses

Most small busines entrepreneurs are merely creating a job for themselves and are most likely to create a profit that supports their family and a modest lifestyle. Small business entrepreneurs usually own and run their own business and hire local employees and family members. Small businesses are the heart of the American economy.

Larger Company Entrepreneurship

Many successful small businesses are eventually acquired by large companies or begin as scalable startups that seek rapid expansion and are capable of attracting investors to provide the capital they need.

In addition to capital they require the expertise of experienced leadership which often comes from C-level executives. The dream of most small business founders is to go large.

Whether you are going to own and operate a brick-and-mortar business or a virtual business the process is the same. You start with an idea. Take the "Benjamin Franklin" approach to do a quick-and-dirty analysis of your business idea.

Take a blank sheet of paper and make a one-page summary of your business idea on the front side. On the back side draw a vertical line down the center dividing the page into two sides. On the top of the left side put a "+" sign and on the top of the right side put a "-"sign. List all of the positive factors on the left side of the page and list all of the negative factors on the right side of the back side of your page.

Beyond that simple exercise, it would probably make sense to engage the services of a professional advisor to save you time and money.

MY ADVICE TO ASPIRING
ENTREPRENEURS
THINKING OF STARTING
THEIR OWN BUSINESS IS:
START SMALL BUT
ALWAYS THINK BIG.

— SIR RICHARD BRANSON

ELEVEN
ADVISORS

Wall Street is the only place that people ride to in a Rolls Royce to get advice from those who take the subway.

— Warren Buffett

How is a Trusted Advisor different than a "Mentor" or "Business Coach"?

Advisors are the wizards or magicians who will ultimately inform, inspire and help the **Innovators**, **Investors,** and **Entrepreneurs** will mold the **C19 Economy** into one unlike any before. Now more than ever Americans need advice they can trust from professionals who are experienced, passionate, and ethical.

There are three opportunities for trusted advisors in the **New Economy**. **First**, there is approximately $70,000,000,000 (with a T) of wealth transferring from baby boomers to their heirs in the next twenty years. The benefactors of this **great wealth transfer** will want advisors from their own peer groups.

Second there are going to be increasing opportunities for advisors who speak both English and Spanish and understand the Latino community. As Asian investors keep away from United States real estate there will be an enormous wave of investors coming from **Latin America** to invest in income properties in Latino communities in the United States.

Third is the unpresented demand for advisors in the **small and medium business** space

The Advisors emerging from the pandemic are entirely different that pre-pandemic advisors. They are tempered by a bitter year of challenges during which they have learned how to reinvent themselves and thrive in a virtual world. Now they are going to take their virtual advisory services viral.

If you are an Advisor — or want to be — this is the time to position yourself with Zombie individuals and Zombie companies that are crying out for help.

At the end of the day your talent and experience have tremendous value. All you need to do is to monetize yourself. Remember the "Call Girl Principle": the value of any service is worth infinitely more *before* it is performed than *after*. In other words, get your money up front. Maybe the most difficult thing about being a consultant or advisor is getting paid. As altruistic as you may be you need to get paid.

We cannot build our own future without helping others to build theirs.

— Bill Clinton

TWELVE
THE MAGIC OF SELLING

You call yourself a salesman, you son of a bitch?

— Blake (Alec Baldwin)
Glengarry Glen Ross (1992)

YOU are the real Magic of Selling!

THE MAGIC OF SELLING

Whoever you are and whatever you do — elotero, paletero, investor, entrepreneur, or advisor — you are selling something to someone.

Selling should be magical. Selling should be an amazing experience for everyone involved.

A Google search of the word "selling" returns about 8,160,000,000 results in 0.52 seconds. It seems like there are unlimited books, seminars, courses, and other sources of information (and misinformation) about the art of selling. Many of you have invested hundreds — if not thousands — of dollars on sales training. Some of you have sales coaches for one reason or another.

The bottom line is that YOU are the magic of selling — YOU are the product (or should be). If you can't sell yourself you can't sell anything.

So how do you discover the magic of selling that you have inside you — your God-given talent and skills?

THE MAGIC OF SELLING

First of all, you have to believe in yourself. You have to believe that you're the greatest salesperson in the world. You have to believe that you can sell anything to anyone (as in sell a Popsicle® to an Eskimo).

Selling can be the worse experience for some — and the best for others. The single determining factor between bad and good is simple — whether you like selling. No, scratch that, it's whether you LOVE selling.

Latinos are natural salespeople because it is a survival skill that is honed by necessity at a very young age. It's very simple — if you want something you must figure out a way to get it.

Like there is no actual Latino stereotype there is no real stereotypical salesperson. Each of us has our own signature style (or we should have). So how do you discover your selling skills and continually improve them? There is only one way and that is to simply start selling. Selling can be extremely simple or extremely complex. It is best to keep selling as simple as you can.

THE MAGIC OF SELLING

How is selling to Latinos any different than selling to non-Latinos? It's not! Forget about everything that marketing gurus want you to believe about "the Latino Market". Latinos are not ignorant and are certainly not any less sophisticated than any other buyers.

But there are some very critical things that you must completely understand about Latinos before you get too excited about selling them anything.

There are major regional differences — even within countries, states, and counties (departments). Those differences are usually reflected in food and music preferences, language dialects —and often in more subtle ways like customs and traditions.

To be uber successful you need to invest the time and effort (and sometimes money) to learn the difference between a tortilla and an arepa —and the difference between salsa and bachata. You need to understand the difference between a fresa and a *fresa*.

A great quote about the importance of self-belief in yourself — and can be applied to your selling skills — comes from the J.M. Barrie (the author of *Peter Pan*): "The moment you doubt whether you can fly, you cease forever to be able to do it."

Think about it. The real magic of selling is your belief in yourself. It's simple. If you believe you can sell then you cal sell. If you don't believe you can sell then you can't sell.

Remember the main reason that Latinos are great salespeople is that stories and emotions sell. Latinos are natural storytellers — and no one group of people understands the power of emotions better than Latinos.

There are 52 Badass Strategies in the next chapter that will help you use the power of emotions and the magic of storytelling to sell a paleta to a paletero or an elote to an elotero. Also, order a copy of *The Magic of Selling* from Amazon.com and maybe a copy of *Rainmaking* (both by Robert Miller.

It's important to
remember that we all
have magic inside us.

— J.K. Rowling

THIRTEEN
STRATEGIES

You outwork, outthink, outscheme and outmanuever. You make no friends. You trust nobody. And you make damn sure you're the smartest guy in the room whenever the subject of money comes up.

— Uncle Pat (Ron Dean)
Cocktail (1988)

You will find some of these strategies and others in *"Rainmaking: Impacting the World Through the Power of Emotions," "The Magic of Selling,"* and *"C19 Economics."* Create a Playbook with your own strategies.

52
BADASS
Strategies
for
LATINO
INVESTORS
ENTREPRENEURS
& ADVISORS

1
FUGGEDABOUTIT!

"Forget about it" is, like, if you agree with someone, you know, like "Raquel Welch is one great piece of ass. Forget about it!" But then, if you disagree, like "A Lincoln is better than a Cadillac? Forget about it!" You know? But then, it's also like if something's the greatest thing in the world, like, "Minghia! Those peppers! Forget about it!" But it's also like saying "Go to hell!" too. Like, you know, like "Hey Paulie, you got a one-inch pecker? And Paulie says "Forget about it!" Sometimes it just means "Forget about it."

— Donnie Brasco (Johnny Depp)
Donnie Brasco (1997)

Minghia!

FUGGEDABOUTIT!

What I need to forget about.

2
HAVE A STRATEGY

Hope is not a strategy.

— Vince Lombardi

So how can you create a strategy when there are no more valid economic principles? Start out with your "why". Why do you want to do <u>anything</u>? Do you want to make millions of dollars? Do you want to save the manatees? Do you want to create financial security for yourself and your family?

Watch Simon Sinek's YouTube Video "Start with Why." Then think about this line from Lewis Carroll's "Alice in Wonderland":

"For, you see, so many out-of-the-way things had happened lately, that Alice had begun to think that very few things indeed were really impossible."

HAVE A STRATEGY

What's my strategy?

3
OUTFOX THEM

We sure outfoxed them.

— Felix the Cat

Felix the Cat, created as a cartoon character in the silent film era, has innate human traits, emotions, and intentions and is a master of psychology and gamesmanship.

The surrealistic situations that Felix faced are much like what we are going through now. The iconic cat with his black body, white face, enormous eyes, and big grin gets out of one mess after another.

Felix always carried his "Magic Bag of Tricks" that he used to outfox his opponents.

OUTFOX THEM

How I outfox them.

4
KNOW YOUR VALUE

A bad salesman will automatically drop his price. Bad salesmen make me sick.

— Sam Stone (Danny DeVito)
Ruthless People (1966)

What is your time worth? How much would you have to make an hour for it not to be worthwhile for you to stop and bend down to pick up a $100 bill on the sidewalk?

Let us say you want to make $1,000,000 a year working 20 hours a week for fifty weeks. That is a thousand hours which means that you need to make a $1,000 per hour (1000 x $1,000 = $1,000,000.

Keep reminding yourself what you are worth. If you do not value your time nobody will.

KNOW YOUR VALUE

What's my value?

_____

_____

_____

_____

_____

_____

_____

_____

_____

_____

_____

_____

_____

_____

_____

_____

_____

_____

_____

_____

5
DEFINE WHO YOU ARE

By God, I shall be a king. This is the time of King Arthur. When we shall — reach for the stars! This is the time of King Arthur when violence is not strength and compassion is not weakness.

— King Arthur (Richard Harris)
Camelot (1967)

Forget the "elevator pitch" and sixty-second commercial that you proudly recite at networking meetings. You know. It is the one that starts out with: "I help people...". Be creative and create something you own.

DEFINE WHO YOU ARE

Who I am.

6

DECIDE WHAT YOU'RE SELLING

The only thing you've got in this world is what you can sell.

— Arthur Miller
Death of a Salesman (1949)

What are you selling (or trying to sell)? Is it a product or service, or both?

One of the biggest reasons for business failure is not selling the right products and services at the right time and at the right price.

Think about the menu at your favorite restaurant. What entices you to order the individual items listed on that menu? Are there too little offerings; or way too many (like a deli menu)? How important are the descriptions? How does price influence your ordering? You should be a "virtual menu" of products and services that constantly changes.

DECIDE WHAT YOU'RE SELLING

What I am selling.

7
KNOW WHAT YOU'RE DEALING WITH

You may think you know what you're dealing with, but, believe me, you don't.

— Noah Cross (John Huston)
Chinatown (1974)

Like war, business is all about creating and executing winning strategies. But before you can create a strategy you must perform your due diligence and know what you are up against. If nothing else, the pandemic has taught us that anything can happen. It has completely redefined "Murphy's Law" (anything that can go wrong will go wrong).

Always know exactly what you are dealing with and all the possible scenarios that may possible play out. Have worst-case scenarios and best-case scenarios, and all the scenarios in between. Keep it as simple as possible. And remember that situations are changing.

KNOW WHAT YOU'RE DEALING WITH

What I am dealing with.

8

KNOW WHO YOU'RE DEALING WITH

If you're playing a poker game and you look around the table and can't tell who the sucker is, it's you.

— Paul Newman

How do you know who you are dealing with? These days its pretty easy to find out about people and companies. Most people start with Google and then search social media.

You can always deep dive by using one of those online services that provides a report of public information. Most professional licenses can be searched online for free and will disclose license status, expiration date, and any restrictions and disciplinary actions.

If you have an opportunity to get "up close and personal" with people, you can appraise body language and other "tells" to get a feeling of who you are dealing with.

KNOW WHO YOU'RE DEALIN

Who I am dealing with.

9

CREATE YOUR EMOTIONAL BRAND

Your brand is what people say about you when you're not in the room.

— Jeff Bezos

The operative word here is "emotional". "Branding" has been a buzz word for a long time. But without emotion a brand means nothing.

Let's think about some brands. One of the most iconic emotional brands in the world is Disney. Many of us have an emotional attachment to Mickey Mouse ears and it's estimated that there have been over 100 million of them sold. And that is not counting the images of them on other merchandise. Mickey Mouse is of the most powerful emotional brands ever created — along with the Playboy Bunny!

CREATE YOUR EMOTIONAL BRAND

My Emotional Brand

10
BE THE EXPERT

Be so good that they can't ignore you.

— Steve Martin

Strategy #6 is "Decide What You Are Selling" and whatever that is you need to be THE expert at that product or service.

Experts always have an opinion and express it with clarity and conviction. After stating your opinion say: "and most of the other EXPERTS agree with ME". BAM!

Obviously, we all cannot be experts at everything. You know the saying "Jack of all trades — Master of none". Choose ONE thing that you want to do better than anyone else and do everything you can to be THE EXPERT. Expertise is comprised of knowledge, talent, and experience. Invest in yourself and obtain knowledge and develop your talent.

BE THE EXPERT

My Expertise

11
BE THE PRODUCT

You are the product. You feeling something. That's what sells. Not them. Not sex. They can't do what we do, and they hate us for it.

— Don Draper (Jon Hamm)
Mad Men (Season 2)

People buy YOU. People choose to do business with you because the like and trust you. Pure and simple.

But here is the one caveat. Draw the line between "like and trust" and "friendship". If you need a friend get a Cocker Spaniel. One of the biggest mistakes many salespeople make is trying to be "friends" with their prospects and clients.

Emotionally distance yourself from your clients. Be the product but do not try to be their friend and definitely not their dog.

My Product

12
GET ON THE COVER

We'll, we're big rock singers We got golden
fingers
And were loved everywhere we go… (That
sounds like us)
We sing about beauty and we sing about
truth
At ten thousand dollars a show . . . (Right)
We take all kinds of pills that give us all
kinds of thrills
But the thrill we've never known Is the thrill
that'll getcha when you get your picture
On the cover of the Rollin' Stone

— Dr. Hook
The Cover of the Rolling Stone (1972)
Shel Silverstein

**These days you do not need to get on the
cover of *Rolling Stone* but you need a
uniquesocial media presence. Position your
emotional brand on social media and on your
own website.**

GET ON THE COVER

Me on the cover of _____.

13
IMAGINE

I hope that we never lose sight of one thing — that it all started with a mouse.

— Walt Disney

Imagine your role in the New Economy and how you are going to impact the world as an Investor, Entrepreneur, or Advisor.

Imagination is vital to the success of capitalism. Whatever we can imagine we can find a way to create. America was virtually built through imagination. People from all over the world arrived here imagining a life of freedom and prosperity.

Our New Economy will be created through our own imaginations. Imagine!

IMAGINE

Imagine

KEEP THE CUSTOMER SATISFIED

14
KEEP THE CUSTOMER SATISFIED

And it's the same old story
Everywhere I go I get slandered, libeled
I hear words I never heard in the Bible
And I'm so tired I'm oh, so tired
But I'm trying to keep my customers
    satisfied
Satisfied

— Paul Simon
Keep the Customer Satisfied (1969)
Paul Simon

**This is a simple strategy that everyone talks
about and many brag about but its easier said
than done.**

**The customer is not always right but that is not
the most important thing. What matters is the
customer experience. It is not about notepads
and calendars, fresh-baked chocolate chip
cookies, or stupid chachkies.**

KEEP THE CUSTOMER SATISFIED

How I Keep Them Satisfied

15
BE EXTRAORDINARY

The thing about Hitchcock which is quite extraordinary for a director of that time, he had a very strong sense of his own image and publicizing himself. Just a very strong sense of himself as the character of Hitchcock.

— Toby Jones

Being "extraordinary" does not mean being a contrarian, weird, or eccentric. It does not mean wearing pink ties (although there is nothing wrong with that) or loud plaid suits (no comment).

How then can you be extraordinary? Like the chicken and the egg the question might be whether you are born extraordinary or become extraordinary. Those who are extraordinary will create tremendous wealth.

BE EXTRAORDINARY

I Am Extraordinary

16
SUPERSIZE YOUR DREAMS

I started out mopping the floor just like you guys. But now… now I'm washing lettuce. Soon I'll be on fries; then the grill. And pretty soon, I'll make assistant manager, and that's when the big bucks start rolling in.

> — Maurice (Louie Anderson)
> *Coming to America* (1988)

Always supersize or "Go Big." Always. All dreams are relative. We all have them, and they come and go during our lifetimes. Hold on tight to your dreams — all of them.

In 2007 Donald Trump published "Think Big and Kick Ass: In Business and in Life". Thinking big worked for Donald Trump and it can work for you.

SUPERSIZE YOUR DREAMS

My Supersized Dreams

_____

_____

_____

_____

_____

_____

_____

_____

_____

_____

_____

_____

_____

_____

_____

_____

_____

_____

_____

_____

17

SELL THEM THEIR DREAMS

'Sell them their dreams,' a woman radio announcer urged a convention of display men in 1923. 'Sell them what they longed for and hoped for and almost despaired of having. Sell them hats by splashing sunlight across them. Sell them dreams — dreams of country clubs and proms and visions of what might happen if only. After all, people don't buy things to have things. They buy things to work for them. They buy hope — hope of what your merchandise will do for them. Sell them this hope and you won't have to worry about selling them goods.

— William R. Leach
Land of Desire

This one is a simple strategy. Do not try to sell people what YOU want to sell. Do not try to sell your dreams. Sell THEIR dreams. Ask "what are your dreams?" and listen.

How I Sell Them Their Dreams

18
WRITE A BOOK

It's a thousand pages, give or take a few. I'll be writing more in a week or two. I could make it longer if you like the style. I can change it 'round. And I want to be a paperback writer. Paperback writer.

— The Beatles
Paperback Writer (1966)
John Lennon and Paul McCartney

Why write a book? A book says a lot about its author. It says that the author took initiative, made a commitment, and saw it through. Contrary to what you may think writing a book is not as easy as it may sound. But it is doable be if you do it right.

A self-published paperback book can be an inexpensive and highly effective way to promote yourself. And you can also publish it digitally as a Kindle Book or other eBook.

WRITE A BOOK

My Book Title: _____

19
TRUST WHO YOU ARE

After a while, you learn to ignore the names people call you and just trust who you are.

— Shrek (Mike Myers)
Shrek (2001)

The more you do or try to do the more people will trash talk about you. Fuggedaboutit! It does not matter. If you did not learn anything else during this shutdown you should have learned "not to sweat the small stuff" and that it is all small stuff.

Trust who you are. Believe unconditionally in yourself. That does not mean that you should be an arrogant narcissistic psychopath, but you must believe in yourself and your vision. Wherever you find spiritual strength, rely on that to constantly remind yourself who you are and why you get up each day. Make every moment count.

Why I Trust Myself

20
STAY FOCUSED

Stay focused, go after your dreams and keep moving toward your goals.

— LL Cool J

Veteran race car drivers quickly learn that they must always keep the "pedal to the metal" no matter what happens on the track. When rookie drivers see an accident on the course they automatically lift their feet off the accelerator pedal out of a sense of self-preservation. It is a natural reflex. When champion drivers see a crash on the course, they push their feet down harder because they know that most of the other drivers will probably be lifting theirs.

Like Seabiscuit, act as if you always are wearing blinders. Do not let anything get between you and the finish line.

How I stay focused

21
CREATE YOUR OWN WORLD

If I had a world of my own, everything would be nonsense. Nothing would be what it is, because everything would be what it isn't. And, contrary wise, what is, it wouldn't be. And, what is wouldn't be, it would. You see?

— *Alice*
Alice's Adventure in Wonderland (1865)
Lewis Carroll

When you think about it we all create our own individual worlds every day. Create a wonderful world of opportunity, challenge, and achievement. Create your own world of wealth, health, and happiness.

The world you create can be beautiful or ugly. It can be fantasy or reality.

CREATE YOUR OWN WORLD

My Own World

22
SURPRISE THEM

You don't understand. I want to be surprised…astonish me, sport, new info, don't care where or how you get it, just get it…

— Gordon Gekko (Michael Douglas)
Wall Street (1987)

"The element of surprise" is a key strategy of war. There are good surprises and bad surprises. Some people like surprises and others hate them. Either way surprises get attention.

Surprise people with GOOD surprises. Under promise and overdeliver. Create value by making people believe they are getting more than they are bargaining for. Astonish people. Dazzle them. Walk them across Pont Neuf, down the Champs Champs-Élysées, or up the Montmartre.

151

SURPRISE THEM

How I Surprise Them

23
SEDUCE THEM

I appreciate this whole seduction thing you've got going on here but let me give you a tip: I'm a sure thing.

— Vivian Ward (Julia Roberts)
Pretty Woman (1990)

Business is all about seduction. It starts at the first moment that you engage a client and should continue throughout the relationship. The moment that you stop seducing them you will start losing them.

Seduction is an art and it is something that you can't learn. Like charisma you either have it or you do not. But do not be discouraged. We all have some God-given "game" and it is just a matter of how, when, and why we choose to develop and use it.

SEDUCE THEM

How I seduce them.

24
ACT AS IF

There's an important phrase that we have here, and think it's time that you all learned it. Act as if. You understand what that means? Act as if you are the fucking President of this firm. Act as if you got a 9" cock. Okay? Act as if.

— Jim Young (Ben Affleck)
Boiler Room (2000)

Have you ever taken an acting class? Method acting is a technique in which an actor aspires to achieve complete emotional identification with a role.

So, you are going to "act as if" what?

ACT AS IF

I Act As If…

_____

_____

_____

_____

_____

_____

_____

_____

_____

_____

_____

_____

_____

_____

_____

_____

25

MAKE A GRAND ENTRANCE

Neither of the two people in the room paid any attention to the way I came in, although only one of them was dead.

— Raymond Chandler
The Big Sleep (1946)

Whether physically or virtually always make a grand entrance. And that applies to arriving at an event or entering a Zoom or Facebook Messenger Room.

What does that even mean? It means walking in with "attitude" or making a powerful opening remark. Making a "grand entrance" is not something that comes easily or even naturally. It requires lots of practice.

MAKE A GRAND ENTRANCE

My Grand Entrance

_____

_____

_____

_____

_____

_____

_____

_____

_____

_____

_____

_____

_____

_____

_____

_____

_____

_____

26
KEEP IT REAL

Listen, Sherlock. While you were tucked away up here working on your ethics, I was out there busting my hump in the REAL world. And the reason guys like you got a place to teach is 'cause guys like me donate buildings.

— Thorton Melon (Rodney Dangerfield)
Back to School (1986)

Unfortunately, we live in a world of bullshit. And there has never been more of it tossed around than during this shutdown. Bullshit from every local, state, and federal governmental agency. Bullshit from the mainstream media. Bullshit all over social media. Bullshit everywhere.

These days everyone is a self-proclaimed medical or financial expert. There are coaches and gurus everywhere. And now they have all gone virtual. Keep it real!

KEEP IT REAL

How I keep it real.

27
DON'T LET THEM FOOL YOU

Never be distracted by people's glamorous portraits of themselves and their lives; search and dig for what really imprisons them.

— Robert Greene
The 48 Laws of Power (1998)

It is the "Facebook Syndrome" — everyone posts pictures at expensive restaurants or in front of expensive cars that may or may not be theirs. "Here in my garage." by Tai Lopez is an example of marketing genius.

DON'T LET THEM FOOL YOU

Why I can't be fooled.

28
CREATE YOUR VISUAL STYLE

Create your own visual style… let it be unique for yourself and yet identifiable for others.

— Oscar Wilde

We live in a visual world. Visual always trumps Verbal. People judge us more by how we look than by what we say. So how do you create your own visual style. Visual style is composed of several factors including how you dress and how you move. Everything you wear, carry, or drive sends messages in addition to your facial expressions and other visual "tells."

Like an actor in makeup and wardrobe you should carefully craft your visual style to portray the right messages at the right time. Your visual style should be agile and not static. Be creative and flexible.

CREATE YOUR VISUAL STYLE

My Visual Style

29
PICK YOUR PARTNERS

My father taught me many things here – he taught me in this room. He taught me: keep your friends close, but your enemies closer.

— Michael Corleone (Al Pacino)
The Godfather, Part II (1974)

Strategic or business partners are one of the most significant aspects of business. Although you cannot do everything by yourself there are situations where you might be better going solo. Partners can either be assets or liabilities.

Concerning business partners, you need to be able to trust them and be convinced that the partnership will be fair to all parties involved. If you form strategic alliances or have "referral partners' proceed with caution.

PICK YOUR PARTNERS

My Partners

30
LOOK FOR THE NEXT COW

I don't like looking back. I'm always constantly looking forward. I'm not the one to sit and cry over spilt milk. I'm too busy looking for the next cow.

— Gordon Ramsey

Always be looking to the next deal. Do not permanently attach yourself to anything or anybody. Marriages are for romantic relationships and not for business ones.

Be quick to forget about the past and quicker to move on. Especially now there are so many deals and clients that you have choices — lots of them. And there are going to be increasingly more as the New Economy unfolds.

Create a DEAL SHEET and stay on the outlook for any deals that may match your parameters. Remain open minded.

My Next Cow

31
SELF-CORRECT

If one dream dies, dream another dream. If you get knocked down, get back up and go again.

— Joel Osteen

Piloting a small airplane requires constant corrections to speed, direction, and altitude. Commercial aircraft are equipped with autopilot devices that are used to guide the planes without direct assistance from pilots. Autopilots maintain airspeed, keep the aircraft straight and level at the proper altitude, and keep it on the correct heading.

We all have an internal autopilot that is a combination of intuition and conscience. Allow your internal autopilot to guide your actions and keep you on course.

SELF-CORRECT

How I self-correct.

32
ASK

Most people never pick up the phone, most people never ask. And that's what separates, sometimes, the people that do things from the people that just dream about them. You gotta act. And you gotta be willing to fail. If you're afraid of failing, you won't get very far.

— Steve Jobs

Ask for the order! Some people are like cowboys who ride around all day and round up cattle and herd them into the corral. The problem is that they do not know how to shut the gate and keep it shut once they get the cattle inside.

You can have strategies, leads, CRMs, sales funnels, coaches, and mentors. But if you don't take action and pick up the phone and ask for the order you will consistently fail.

ASK

Why I'm not afraid to ask.

33
MANAGE YOUR REPUTATION

Your brand name is only as good as your reputation.

— Richard Branson

At the end of each day and at the end of our lives what do we really have? All we have is our reputation. Our reputation is our legacy — and that legacy can be good or bad.

Managing your reputation and "protecting your name" can be challenging especially when you are a risk-taker. The more aggressive and the more active you are the more open you are to criticism, trash-talking, and personal and business attacks on your reputation.

Without becoming paranoid or paralyzed monitor your reputation and manage it to the best of your ability. Google yourself and be on the lookout for false information.

My Reputation

34
TAKE RISKS

The biggest risk is not taking any risk... In a world that's changing really quickly, the only strategy that is guaranteed to fail is not taking risks.

— Mark Zuckerberg

So, after that warning about managing your reputation do not let anything keep you from taking risks.

There are frivolous risks and there are calculated risks. Frivolous risks are based on emotions and calculated risks are based on reason. Most risks involve a combination of both— in varying proportions.

As we grow older we tend to program ourselves to be risk adverse. But, as toddlers learning to walk, we have a natural tendency to stand up every time we stumble and fall.

TAKE RISKS

My Risk Tolerance

35
BE WHERE THE PUCK IS GOING

I skate to where the puck is going to be,
not where it has been.

— Wayne Gretzky

"The Great One" always skates to where the puck is going. Be like the great one. You don't want to be where the puck is and especially not where the puck was. Be where the puck is going.

Unless you believe in psychic readers, mediums, and crystal balls the coming weeks, months and years will probably be the most challenging of our lifetimes.

Forget about traditional fundamental and technical analysis. Dramatically change the way you think. And stop acting entirely logically and start increasingly acting based on the emotions of The New Economy.

BE WHERE THE PUCK IS GOING

Where the Puck Is Going

36
VISUALIZE THE DEAL

I would visualize things coming to me. It would just make me feel better. Visualization works if you work hard. That's the thing. You can't just visualize and go eat a sandwich.

— Jim Carrey

This is not as easy as it sounds — and involves much more than making a vision board with magazine cut-outs of a Ferrari and Newport Coast Mansion.

VISUALIZE THE DEAL

How I visualize my deals.

37
STOP PLEASING OTHERS

Alice, you cannot live your life to please others. The choice must be yours because when you step out to face that creature, you will step out alone.

— White Queen (Anne Hathaway)
Alice in Wonderland (2010)

Stop pleasing others. Do not be a doormat and the object of other peoples' displaced anger.

Many of us have learned that the clients we give the most seem like the ones from whom we realize the lowest return on investment. Conversely, we usually make the most money on the clients that are the less needy and are without unnecessary drama and complications.

STOP PLEASING RULES

Why I'm not a pleaser.

38
STOP FOLLOWING RULES

You don't learn to walk by following rules. You learn to walk by doing, and by falling over.

— Richard Branson

Like badges, we don't need no stinkin' rules. Stop following rules. Challenge rules. The only rules are that there are no rules.

Obviously, there are some rules that you should follow like stopping at a red light and paying your taxes. But most other rules are roadblocks to your success.

You have the freedom to determine exactly which rules you choose to follow — and exactly which rules you choose to challenge or ignore. Push against rules and push as hard as you can to constantly redefine them. The 26 Badass Rules in this book are exceptions.

STOP FOLLOWING RULES

Me & Rules

39
BE A CINDERELLA STORY

Cinderella story. Outta nowhere. A former greenskeeper, now, about to become the Masters champion. It looks a miracle… It's in the hole! It's in the hole! It's in the hole!

Carl Spackler (Bill Murray)
Caddyshack (1980)

Almost everyone loves a "Cinderella Story." We love *"Beauty and the Beast"* and *"Harry Potter"* and *"The Wizard of Oz"* and *"Alice in Wonderland"* and *"Peter Pan"*. What is our favorite land in Disneyland? Most of us love Fantasyland.

Make your life a fairy tale. Make it a Cinderella Story. Create your Pumpkin Coach and ride it to the most exciting and prosperous place it can take you. It is easy. All you must do is dream and believe. Reach for the stars — all of them — and always wash your hands for lunch.

BE A CINDERELLA STORY

My Cinderella Story

40

CREATE HYPE — BUT DON'T BELIEVE IT

My own saying is: 'Create the hype, but don't ever believe it.'

— Simon Cowell

Never ever drink the Kool-Aid. You can mix it up and serve it. You can believe that it works. But never ever drink it.

There are salespeople who believe the hype they are fed. One of the biggest examples of this occurs in the world of network marketing.

All those life insurance marketing organizations with three-letter acronyms that claim to be "helping people" or "educating people" are like religious cults. They have people drinking every flavor of Kool-Aid and salivating for certificates and rings and trips. Avoid drinking the Kool-Aid and avoid forcing it on others.

CREATE HYPE — BUT DON'T BELIEVE IT

Why I don't drink the Kool-Aid.

41
BELIEVE

The moment you doubt whether you can fly, you cease for ever to be able to do it.

— J.M. Barrie
Peter Pan (1904)

This is the most amazing strategy. It is amazingly simple but extremely difficult to achieve. We all know the story of the four-minute mile. We know the story of the Wright Brothers and their quest for manned flight. But many of us choose to be doubters and haters instead of simply just believing.

Jules Verne believed in going to the moon and journeying under the sea. He believed in travelling around the world in eighty days. Walt Disney believed in his little mouse. Steve Jobs believed in his "computer." Elon Musk believes. So does every successful entrepreneur — the unsuccessful ones stopped believing somewhere along the road.

My Beliefs

42
MAKE AN OFFER

Michael Corleone: My father made him an offer he couldn't refuse.
Kay Adams: What was that?
Michael Corleone: Luca Brasi held a gun to his head, and my father assured him that either his brains or his signature would be on the contract.
Kay Adams: …
Michael Corleone: …That's a true story.

— *The Godfather* (1972)

Always make an offer. It may not be the right offer, but you always must make an offer. And do not play games. Make your offer one time and hold fast to that offer.

What is an offer they cannot refuse? Make your best offer based on a fair deal. Do not waste your time with ridiculous back and forth negotiations that go nowhere.

My Negotiating Style

43

PRESS HARD — THERE ARE 3 COPIES

Only one thing counts in this world: Get them to sign on the line that is dotted.

— Blake (Alec Baldwin)
Glengarry Glen Ross (1992)

There is one and only one objective to every deal — getting it done as quickly as possible. Keep things simple. Find out what they want and determine whether you can deliver.

If you cannot get them to sign the deal then nothing else matters. Before the digital age when people were signing contracts, salespeople would tell their clients "press hard — there are 3 copies."

What is the quickest and easiest way to get them to "sign on the line that is dotted"? Do not waste time. Present an offer and ask for the business <u>once</u>. Either the answer will be "yes" or "no." Move on!

My Closing Style

44
QUESTION AUTHORITY

Fellas… I don't recognize the right of this committee to ask me these kinds of questions. And, furthermore, you can all go fuck yourselves.

— Howard Prince (Woody Allen)
The Front (1996)

Question authority — question everything. We should have learned our lesson from the way that this crisis was mishandled. We were caught off guard and found ourselves in a vulnerable and highly confusing situation.

Finally, people started questioning authority because "authority" lost any credibility that it had. We probably should have questioned authority at the beginning of this crisis — but we did not. Do not become an obnoxious rebel just for the sake of rebellion but question authority.

Me & Authority

45
BE THE LAST COCA-COLA

Anna Maria: He thinks he's the last Coca-Cola in the desert.
Lanna Lake: Honey, he is.

— Anna Maria (Cordella González)
Lanna Lake (Cathy Moriarty)
Mambo Kings (1992)

You are sometimes better to be the last in and first out. That means lay back and let the other fools rush in and chase the business before you jump in. And when you jump in be "the last Coca-Cola in the desert."

What does that mean — "the last Coca-Cola in the desert"? It means that you must present yourself as being entirely irresistible. Who would not want the last Coca-Cola in the desert? How do you make yourself irresistible? Reputation creates demand!

BE THE LAST COCA-COLA

Why I'm the last Coca-Cola.

46
BE EXCLUSIVE

You want to know how to get people to trust you with their money? I'll tell you right now. You present it as an exclusive thing… Nothing on Earth makes people want something more than telling them they can't have it.

— Bernard Madoff (Richard Dreyfus)
Madoff (2015)

What is the world population? Approaching 8 billion? How many people are there in the United States? Maybe 350 million? How many people in your profession? If you sell real estate there are probably over 2 million people in the United States trying to do the same thing as you. That is 2 million! And there is only 1 of you. Be exclusive. There is only one of you with your unique skills, experience, and passion.

BE EXCLUSIVE

How exclusive am I?

47
HIT HARD — HIT FAST —HIT OFTEN

Hit hard, hit fast, hit often.

— Lt. General Lewis "Chesty" Puller
The United States Marine Corps

Hit hard, hit fast, hit often. A lot of people are using "pivot", but pivoting means absolutely nothing unless you pivot with power, speed, and persistence.

Think about what we have learned from our other strategies. First you must define who you are and know your "why." Second you must know what you are selling — how you plan to sell it — and your target clients. Third you must be innovative and agile. Fourth you must take massive action with power, speed, and persistence.

HIT HARD — HIT FAST — HIT OFTEN

How I hit hard, fast, and often.

48
GIVE THEM WHAT THEY WANT

I want ten chocolate chip cookies. Medium chips. None too close to the outside.

— Howard Hughes (Leonardo DiCaprio)
The Aviator (2004)

This should be the simplest thing for you to do. When someone tells you <u>exactly</u> what they want then find a way to give it to them and determine if you can make money doing it.

"Ten chocolate chip cookies. Medium chips. None too close to the outside." Sounds easy. Why make it any more complicated. Find the cookies. Set a price. Done deal!

If you could do deals like that all day you would be in hog heaven. Find out exactly what people want as quickly as possible — and how much they are willing to pay.

GIVE THEM WHAT THEY WANT

How I give them what they want.

49
FIND THEIR ACHILLES HEEL

Ah, but remember, my friends. Even Tramp has his Achilles heel.

— Boris
Lady and the Tramp (1955)

Achilles was the greatest of all Greek warriors and a hero of the Trojan War. His mother held him by one of his heels to make him invulnerable. The heel did not get covered by water and he was later killed by an arrow wound. That is the myth of the 'Achilles Heel.'

Know your vulnerabilities and especially know the vulnerabilities of your allies and opponents. Leverage off their fear and greed. There is nothing wrong with it. It is not personal — it is just business.

How I find their Achilles Heel.

50
DON'T OVERSELL

You had me at hello.

— Dorothy Boyd (Renee Zellweger)
Jerry Maguire (1996)

The quicker you shut up the more successful you will be. Learn to listen. One of the biggest mistakes many rookie salespeople make is vomiting their enthusiasm all over everyone with whom they come in contact.

Ever been stuck with a life insurance salesperson or trapped in a timeshare presentation? How about a MLM meeting or encounter with a religious zealot?

In the Land of Desire everybody wants to buy — buy nobody wants to be sold. Stop selling! Curb your enthusiasm. Shut up. Listen. Do not make the mistake of talking yourself OUT of a deal. You had them at "Hello."

DON'T OVERSELL

Why I don't oversell.

51
BE BRAVE

'You have plenty of courage, I am sure,' answered Oz. 'All you need is confidence in yourself. There is no living thing that is not afraid when it faces danger. The true courage is in facing danger when you are afraid, and that kind of courage you have in plenty.'

— L. Frank Baum
The Wonderful Wizard of Oz (1900)

What is courage? Unlike charisma which is a priceless gift from God courage can be acquired. How do we build courage in our lives? We build courage from pain, hurt and failing. The more me stumble the more we need courage to get back up. But courage comes from out guts and not our minds.

Why Is the badge for the Life rank in the Boy Scouts a heart?

52
PRAY

I have been driven many times upon my knees by the overwhelming conviction that I had no where else to go. My own wisdom and that of all about me seemed insufficient for that day.

— Abraham Lincoln

Prayer is universal to all religions and beliefs. Sometime prayer is to ask for something — "God help me." And sometimes prayer is for gratitude — "All the praises and thanks be to Allah."

You may call it prayer or meditation or even something else. What is important is that you set some quiet time alone each day when you can think about who you are, what you are doing and, especially, why?

PRAY

Pray

_____

_____

_____

_____

_____

_____

_____

_____

_____

_____

_____

_____

_____

_____

_____

_____

_____

_____

_____

My Favorite Strategies

FOURTEEN
RULES

You are remembered for the rules you
break.

— Douglas MacArthur

**There is a difference —a BIG difference —
between these 26 Badass Rules and the 52
Badass Strategies. The rules are mandatory
and the strategies are optional.**

26

RULES

for

BADASS

LATINO

INVESTORS
ENTREPRENEURS
& ADVISORS

1
CLOSE THE DEAL

Deals are my art form. Other people paint beautifully on canvas or write beautiful poetry. I like making deals, preferably big deals. That's how I get my kicks.

— Ed Koch

Get their money or someone else will.

CLOSE THE DEAL

How I close deals.

_____

_____

_____

_____

_____

_____

_____

_____

_____

_____

_____

_____

_____

_____

_____

_____

_____

_____

_____

_____

_____

_____

2
BE TEFLON

Does your mind feel more and more like Teflon? Nothing sticks to it?

— Lily Tomlin

Ask us about "Teflon Tim".

BE TEFLON

Why nothing can hurt me.

3
DON'T ASSUME ANYTHING

When you assume, you make an *ass* out of *you* and *me*.

— Felix Unger (Tony Randall)
The Odd Couple

You might be safe to assume that "the sun will come up tomorrow" if you believe Little Orphan Annie.

DON'T ASSUME ANYTHING

Why I assume nothing.

4
CHOOSE WORDS WISELY

There are those whose rash words are like sword thrusts, but the tongue of the wise brings healing.

— Proverbs 12:18

If you feel you *must* say something potentially hurtful then "hold your tongue" and count to ten while you evaluate the potential direct and collateral damage.

CHOOSE WORDS WISELY

Words I favor and words I avoid.

5
MAKE SURE IT'S WORTH IT

Two rainbows found they had rainbows on their curves. They flickered out saying: 'It was worth being a bubble, just to have held that rainbow thirty seconds.'

— Carl Sandburg

¿Se vale la pena?

How quickly I figure what's in it for me.

6
BURN BRIDGES

Commitment means burning all bridges behind you.

— Billy Graham

Cut toxic people and situations out of your life and don't look back.

BURN BRIDGES

How I burn bridges.

7
HAVE NO FEAR

Courage isn't having the strength to go on — it is going on when you don't have strength.

— Napoleon Bonaparte

True courage doesn't come from tequila.

HAVE NO FEAR

Por qué no tengo miedo.

8

HAVE THE BALLS TO SAY NO

What you don't do determines what you can do."

— Tim Ferriss

Tequila makes saying "no" much easier.

HAVE THE BALLS TO SAY NO

How I say "no" en Español.

9
LOOK GOOD

It is better to look good than to feel good.

— Fernando Lamas

Always look "rico suave".

LOOK GOOD

How I look *rico suave*.

10
FEEL GOOD

When you look good, you feel good. Confidence with what you're wearing is very important. If you feel good, you will always perform your best without worrying about anything.

— Maria Sharapova

If you don't take care of yourself nobody will.

FEEL GOOD

How I feel *rico suave*.

11
ATTRACT YOUR OWN TRIBE

Whatever you do in life, surround yourself with smart people who'll argue with you.

— John Wooden

Put together your own "A Team".

ATTRACT YOUR OWN TRIBE

This is my tribe.

12
PLAY WELL WITH OTHERS

A lion's work hours are only when he's hungry, once he's satisfied, the predator and the prey live peacefully together.

— Chuck Jones

At least *try* to get along!

PLAY WELL WITH OTHERS

How I play well with others.

13

COLOR OUTSIDE THE LINES

You have to color outside the lines once in a while if you want to make your life a masterpiece.

— Albert Einstein

Color outside the lines and erase as many as you can along the way.

COLOR OUTSIDE THE LINES

When I color outside the lines.

14
ALWAYS HAVE AN OPINION

He who has no opinion of his own, but depends on the opinion and taste of others, is a slave.

— Friedrich Gottlieb Klopstock

Always have an opinion and deliver it with conviction.

ALWAYS HAVE AN OPINION

Why my opinion matters.

15
REACH FOR THE STARS

Everyone needs something to aim for. You can call it a challenge, or you can call it a goal. It is what makes us human. It was challenges that took us from being cavemen to reaching for the stars.

— Richard Branson

Always reach for the stars — all of them.

REACH FOR THE STARS

The stars I reach for.

16
NEVER APOLOGIZE

An apology? Bah! Disgusting! Cowardly! Beneath the dignity of any gentleman, however wrong he might be.

— Steve Martin

Avoid apologizing at all costs — they are usually little more than weak excuses.

NEVER APOLOGIZE

Why I never apologize.

17
SAVE THE CHEAP SALES TALK

Save the cheap salesman talk, will ya? It's obvious.

> — Gordon Gekko
> *Wall Street* (1987)

Don't beg for business. Never use these words and phrases:
Honestly • To be honest • To be completely honest • I want to earn your business • At the end of the day • Please don't hesitate to call • Just following up • What would it take to get your business? • We pride ourselves on • To be truthful with you • To tell you the truth • Frankly • I guarantee it • Trust me •

SAVE THE CHEAP SALES TALK

Why I don't beg for business.

18
BE A TIMESHARE SALESPERSON

The slick, fast-talking, time-share salesman still exists. He may no longer wear a lime-green leisure suit, but he's solely focused on the sale — and he's largely the reason the industry has a less-than-stellar reputation.

— Lisa Ann Schreier

Relentless.

BE A TIMESHARE SALESPERSON

What I know about the timeshare pitch.

19
BE A HIJO DE PUTA

Bad luck doesn't have any chinks in it.
I was born a son of a bitch and I am going
to die a son of a bitch.

— Captain Rogue Carnicero
One Hundred Years of Solitude
Gabriel García Márquez

It's not necessarily bad!

BE A HIJO DE PUTA

Why?

20
NO BUSINESS CARDS

Rock stars get room keys, I get business cards.

— Thomas Friedman

Collect business cards. Don't have any to give out. Better to share a contact from your smartphone or have a digital card.

NO BUSINESS CARDS

What I do with cards I collect.

21
NO POSERS, FAKERS, OR WANNABEES

A life of praying means death to every identity that does not come from God."

— Brennan Manning
Posers, Fakers, and Wannabees:
Unmasking the Real You

Badass Latinos, like Badass Investment Bankers, are not self-proclaimed.

DON'T BE A POSER

What's the REAL you?

22
LUNCH IS FOR WIMPS

Lunch? Ahh, you gotta be kidding. Lunch is for wimps.

> — Gordon Gekko (Michael Douglas)
> *Wall Street* (1987)

It's an urban legend that deals get done at lunch.

LUNCH IS FOR WIMPS

Why I don't "DO" lunch.

23
NO STINKING BADGES

Badges, the god-damned hell with badges! We have no badges! In fact, we don't have to show you any stinking badges, you god-damned cabrón and chinga tu madre.

— Gold Hat (Alfonso Bedoya)
The Treasure of the Sierra Madre (1927)

Translate: cabrón and chinga tu madre.

NO STINKING BADGES

Why I wear a badge.

24
LOOK 'EM IN THE EYE

Your eyes are like two jewels in the sky.

— Bob Dylan

The eyes are windows to the soul.

LOOK 'EM IN THE EYE

My technique for "looking 'em in the eye".

25
REMEMBER THEIR NAME

I nicknamed everybody in the gym. It was easier than remembering their name.

— Joe Gold

Their name is the most important thing that people have. Ask people their name and repeat it. If it is strange to you ask them to repeat it and then pronounce it yourself. Spell their name and repeat the pronunciation. Ask them how you did.

REMEMBER THEIR NAME

How I remember names.

26
STOP STINKING THINKING

Positive thinking won't let you do anything other than bring more positive thinking into your mind. Into your experience, into your life, into your business, into your relationships, into everything that you do. Stop "stinking thinking".

— Zig Ziglar

The American psychologist Albert Ellis is credited with coining the phrase *"stinking thinking'* to describe the human tendency to persistently engage with thoughts that do not serve us.

STOP STINKING THINKING

How I'll stop stinking thinking.

MY FAVORITE RULES

FIFTEEN
TOOLBOX

I don't believe in the kind of magic in my books. But I do believe something very magical can happen when you read a good book.

— J.K. Rowling

Tools in your toolbox, arrows in your quiver, or hacks— whatever you call them — have as many as you can always available.

FELIX THE CAT
had his little
Bag of Tricks
and you have your
Toolbox

60 SECOND SPEECH

Ideas alone are not scalable. Only when a idea is put into words that people can clearly understand can an idea inspire action.

— Simon Sinek

Some call it an elevator speech or 60 second pitch. If you have ever been to a leads group or networking event you have been asked to present one. Most of them sound the same because they begin with: "I help people..."

Why do you do what you do? That's what you should be explaining in your **60 Second Speech**. Do not start out something like "I help people find their dream house…"

Smart people do not want to hear you vomit some canned pitch about how great your products are or how you will do anything to "earn their business" (which usually just means lowering the price).

Then what should you say in 60 short seconds? Passionately share your **WHY**. Something like this: "I believe that there is an optimal financial solution for every deal and I challenge myself to find it by thinking creatively, reaching for the stars, and coloring outside the lines to quickly close deals while providing world class experiences."

Be unique and keep your words at a sixth-grade level. And do not make it sound like a cheap sales pitch. Be confident. Do not sound condescending or patronizing. Perfect yourself by recording videos.

MY 60 SECOND SPEECH

MY 60 SECOND SPEECH

PERSONAL PLAN

A goal without a plan is just a wish.

— Antoine de Saint Exupéry

Create a dynamic digital plan in a Word file so that you continually modify it and easily share it.

PERSONAL PLAN

This is a personal plan — not a business plan. You will create your business plan in the next sections: **Game Plan** and **Playbook**. Think about this **Plan** as a personal flight plan like the ones that pilots prepare and file prior to taking off — indicating the plane's planned route. Flight plans follow a standard format detailing the flight path and include departure and arrival points, estimated flight time, alternate airports in case of bad weather, whether the flight is visual or instrument, name of pilot and crew, passenger list and details about the aircraft.

Invest time and effort into creating your own "flight plan." Keep it simple. Your challenge will not be what to put in; your challenge will be what to leave out. Your plan should be dynamic and flexible.

Keep in mind that this plan is for your own use. It should describe your vision, your "why" and how and when you plan to achieve your dreams. Include **who, what, where, when, how**, and **why**. Create your plan in Word and save it on a flash drive.

MY PERSONAL PLAN

MY PERSONAL PLAN

GAME PLAN

You don't get abs like these eating peanut butter patties.

— Joe Kingman (Dwayne Johnson)
The Game Plan (2007)

We all have dreams, and we should hold on tight to our dreams — all of them. But without a game plan a dream remains nothing more than a dream. And many dreams slowly morph into sudor y pedos before completely disappearing.

A plan without action is useless and action without a plan can be ineffective. You need both to be effective.

GAME PLAN

A Game Plan is more than a business plan. Your game plan is where you visualize your dreams and then record your strategy for achieving them.

Although many of us do not remember his name most of us have heard the story about the POW who spent seven years in a prison cell mentally playing golf. It is the story of combat pilot Major James Nesmeth who was shot down over North Vietnam. Locked in solitary confinement his daily game plan was to play a round of golf in his mind. Every day he imagined getting dressed in his favorite golf clothes, driving to his country club, and playing a round of golf. Because he was playing the game in his head every game was perfect. Not long after returning home to the United States he went to his club and played a real game of golf — his best game ever. Although he had lost a lot of weight and was playing with a body that had deteriorated while in prison, he played his best game ever because his mind was sharp and he followed his rehearsed game plan. Be creative and think big — very **BIG**.

MY GAME PLAN

MY GAME PLAN

PLAYBOOK

The Democrats, the left has this 30-year playbook of how to destroy conservatives by simply exposing the horrible, the mean-spirited, insensitive things they say, but that isn't going to work on Trump the way it works on conservatives, for a whole host of reasons.

— Rush Limbaugh

Constructing your Game Plan was the hard part — making your Playbook is the fun part. Keep it simple and easy to read. Use a lot of graphics and colors. Primarily your playbook should be compelling, complete, organized, and logical. Make it special.

Your **Playbook** should be your most valuable tool. Creating an effective playbook requires a commitment to excellence. Remember that is more than a business plan — it is a play-by-play guide to everything included in your **Game Plan**.

Here is a unique concept for Playbook. Create an account at wix.com and pick a name for your Playbook. You can select a template and build a website to manage your game plan. Your Playbook will be hosted online and you can make it password protected.

Make your Playbook dynamic and fun. It should be a living document that can be modified and improved at any time. Be sure to include **company overview**, **products and services**, **ideal customer profile**, **marketing**, **sales methodology**, **compensation**, and **resources**.

Your Playbook is a work-in-progress that you will update and modify, as necessary. Putting your Playbook online will make it accessible to your entire team at any time.

MY PLAYBOOK

MY PLAYBOOK

PITCH DECK

Investors don't look at pitch decks for very long — just an average of 3 minutes and 44 seconds.

— Tech Crunch
Techcrunch.com

Combine the power of emotions and the magic of storytelling with amazing graphics to create powerful visual presentation. You do not have to be entirely transparent, but you should avoid lying, exaggerating and everything that might be perceived as being deceptive or misleading.

The majority of what we take away from most presentations is **visual**. Your **Pitch Deck** is a public document designed for a multitude of reasons including financing and promoting your idea or company. Ideally you will have several versions of your pitch deck — each with their own specific purpose. You should have one pitch deck for investors and another for presenting your company in conferences or at meetings.

There are several pitch deck templates online that you can reference in order to get some ideas for creating your own. Do not be a copycat. The key to a compelling pitch deck is originality. When writing your pitch deck remember that you can make the most impact through the power of emotions and the magic of storytelling.

The number of slides and average reading time for each version of your pitch deck will depend on the target audience. Investors have shorter attention spans and want to get to the heart of your pitch quickly. Keep it as short and simplest as possible.

MY PITCH DECK

MY PITCH DECK

VIDEOS

I'm a little bit naked, but that's okay.

— Lady Gaga

You're a movie star! Why not? Everyone else is. The key to creating killer videos is quality. Remember that your video directly reflects who you are. And once t has been published you can never take it back so do not share anything that you don't want online forever. Be super creative. Go crazy and have fun. And stay focused on why you are shooting the video in the first place.

VIDEOS

Videos are the best way to tell your story and your story is the best way to raise capital and promote your idea or business. There is an art to making videos and the skills you need can be learned only one way — through trial and error. The more video experience you get the better your videos will be. And the best videos and not the most perfect ones. The best videos are the ones that are candid and real.

Here are a few tips for creating videos:

1. **Use the back camera on your phone.**
2. **Use a solid-colored background.**
3. **Make sure there is plenty of light.**
4. **Use a good microphone for best audio.**
5. **Develop a strong camera presence.**
6. **Experiment with different angles.**
7. **Edit with a app like iMovie.**
8. **Have a script before you begin.**
9. **Aggressively promote your videos.**

Making professional videos will take time — you should create videos and post them on Facebook, YouTube, Instagram, Twitter, and other social media accounts. Make them short, unique, and captivating.

MY VIDEOS

MY VIDEOS

EMOTIONS

Latinos are emotional — extremely emotional. If you do not believe that watch a soccer game or telenovela. If you are a Latino or Latina, you know what we are talking about.

We are trained to think that people act or fail to act for logical reasons. Logic only provides us with confusing (and often conflicting) information. In the end, we are all creatures of emotion. We must retrain ourselves to empathize and to follow our hearts, not our minds.

Emotions make the world go 'round. There are positive emotions and negative emotions, and some emotions (like passion) can play either role. People are guided by their emotions when making decisions. They intake information and process it, but their actions (or lack thereof) are based on what they feel. Learn about the many types of emotions and rank them in the order of importance to you.

EMOTIONS

Emotions can be powerful drivers or enormous roadblocks. The key to leveraging other people's emotions is being in control of your own. It is equally important to empathize with their raw feelings without being patronizing

All our emotions — our feelings — begin in our brain. Our brain, weighing only about three pounds is our most powerful organ. It is made up of several parts that work together to process the information we receive. The part of the brain that regulates our emotions is the *limbic system*.

Our *limbic system* controls our emotions, memories, and stimulation. Our emotions are controlled by the levels of certain chemicals in our brain. Our brain, having the texture of firm jelly, is a complex network which controls information and sends signals via neurotransmitters. Our brain processes the present, memories of past experiences, and preconceived ideas and expectations. Obviously, prescription medications, recreational drugs, alcohol, and even foods affect our emotions.

EMOTIONS

The *amygdala* is an integrative center controlling our motivation, emotions, and emotional behavior. It is the starting point for fear and anxiety, which occur when environmental factors or stressors signal that we are in danger. Here is how the chain reaction works: the stressors signal the amygdala to prepare for 'fight or flight,' and *epinephrine* is released into our bloodstream attempting to keep us safe.

Dopamine is a chemical that is released by nerve cells in our brain and transmitted to other nerve cells in our body. It is a neurotransmitter which plays a significant role in reward-motivated behavior. *Dopamine* is what gives us our feelings of accomplishment when we close a deal or finish a race — it is known as 'the pleasure chemical' that gives us that natural high that we all love and desire.

Serotonin, also a neurotransmitter, is known as 'the calming chemical' and makes us feel focused and relaxed. It is a major contributor to making us feel happy. — that's what all of us want.

EMOTIONS NOTES

Oxytocin, a hormone, is an endorphin which functions as a natural pain reliever which masks pain and helps reduce stress in our body. It gives us a sense of safety and is especially important at the beginning of our relationships.

Cortisol, a steroid hormone, is produced in the adrenal cortex of our brain. It is produced in response to stress or anxiety and functions to increase our blood sugar.

Our emotions are linked to and necessary for all the decisions we make. Without our emotions and feelings, we would be unable to distinguish between rational and irrational behavior. Time also plays an important role: the more quickly we decide, the more confident we feel; the longer it takes, the less confident we feel. Every decision involves emotions at some level.

People act when their emotions tell them to act. That does not mean that using negative emotions to control people is right, but it does mean that you need understand why people make decisions.

STORYTELLING

ONCE UPON A TIME are the four words that begin a lot of stories, but they all have different endings. Exceptional stories not only tell you who, what and when. They tell you why.

Storytelling is an art, not a science. Everyone has their stories, and everyone has their ways of telling them. Some stories are amazing — inspiring delight, pleasure, desire, or admiration. Other stories are terrible — provoking effects that are extremely unpleasant or disagreeable. We all have our own stories

Stories can magically transport you and your emotions to anywhere the storyteller wants to take you. Stories can be straightforward and entertaining, or they can have very profound messages either above or below the surface. Stories can provoke thoughts and actions. Stories must be structured to capture and maintain the reader's or listener's interest.

STORYTELLING

Your success as an entrepreneur depends on your story-making skills. You must be creative, captivating, and credible (with the accent on credible). If people don't believe you, you'll be wasting your time.

In the words of Taylor Swift: "You can draw inspiration from anything. If you're a good storyteller, you can take a dirty look somebody gives you, or if a guy you used to have flirtations with starts dating a new girl, or somebody you're casually talking to says something that makes you so mad — you can create an entire scenario around that."

Make your stories brief and entertaining. Be in tune with your eaudience and aware of how you can make the maximum impact.

Storytelling is vital to growing a business. From sales presentations to pitch-decks for attracting investors storytelling skills are mandatory for all seasoned or aspiring entrepreneurs. Craft your personal story and one for your business. Then perfect the stories through practice.

TELLS

Tells are what people consciously and unconsciously communicate verbally and nonverbally. Tells are indicators of people's emotions, which encompasses their feelings, thoughts, attitudes, and moods. Tells can help you read people at any given moment, including their characteristics and personality traits.

Train yourself to be a people watcher and learn about the "tells" that will help you make your decisions. And take some videos of yourself and analyze your tells.

Words and Phrases

- truthfully, to be truthful with you
- frankly, to be frank with you
- honestly, to be honest with you
- "earn your business"
- actually
- stuttering
- slang
- foreign words
- any profanity

Appearance

• their manner of dress
• personal grooming (nails)
• style and condition of shoes
• jewelry (bling, religious or spiritual artifacts)
• tattoos, piercings, hair styling and coloring

The Voice

• volume, pitch, and tone
• pace, pauses, and variation
• sound frequencies creating vibrations
• control and modulation
• speed — nervously rushed or slowed

Emotional Energy

• the intensity of people's presence
• the strength of a handshake or hug
• gut feelings
• crying
• laughing
• excitement
• intuitive empathy
• anger
• anxiety
• fear
• negative energy

TELLS

Body Language

- eyes — the #1 Tell
- facial expressions and micro expressions
- posture and movements
- the position of the body
- breathing, heartbeat, perspiration, blushing
- the odors emitted by the body
- how and what people touch
- eating and drinking habits and choices
- perceived health and wellness
- hand movements, gestures, positioning

Nervous Habits

- finger tapping and foot tapping
- nail biting and lip biting
- nervous smoking or drinking
- grinding and clenching teeth
- sucking or chewing pens or pencils
- playing with hair (or facial hair)
- cracking knuckles
- touching the face
- uncontrolled laughing or giggling
- coughing
- twitching
- laughing
- stuttering
- darting eyes

There are many different opinions on the role that words, body language, and voice play in the process of communicating. I believe that all three combined account for only one-half of all communication. Here are my estimates: words (5%), body language (25%), and voice (20%). Emotional energy accounts for 50% of people's communication.

Because the face is the most accurate indicator of a person's emotions, Rainmakers must especially master the interpretation of facial expressions (micro expressions). The best way to do that is to look at yourself in the mirror and mimic some facial expressions. When you put an expression on your face, you will begin to feel the emotion. Emotions cause expressions and expressions can cause emotions.

The masks we have been forced to wear during the pandemic make reading micro expressions challenging — and the results are limited. Without being to see the mouth we must focus more on the eyes.

MY STRATEGIC PARTNERS

MY ADVISORS

PERSONAL MOTTO

To see the world, things dangerous to come to, to see behind walls, draw closer, to find each other.

> — Motto of *Life Magazine*
> *The Secret Life of Walter Mitty* (2013)

Many companies have mottos but how many people do you know who have a motto?

MY PERSONAL MOTTO

SIXTEEN
GRINGOS

I don't like gringos at all. They are very boring and all have faces like unbaked rolls.

— Frida Kahlo

Gringo (male) and *gringa* (female) are terms used to describe "foreigner" from the perspectives of Spanish and Portuguese-speaking countries and Latinos in the United States (where it sometimes carries negative connotations). A typical thought or comment might be: "relax pinche cabrón gringo, I'm here legally."

There are many theories about the origin of the term *gringo* and the term has been around for at least a couple of hundred years. Like other words *gringo* and *gringa* can mean pretty much whatever you want them to mean — good, bad, or very, very, ugly.

This is for gringos. You know who you are! For the sake of this chapter a "gringo" is everyone who is *not* a Latino. Having said that, this is probably the most politically incorrect part of our book.

This is not a primer on "Latino Marketing" — it's about doing business with Latinos. We have defined "Latinos" ad nauseum and have defined "Gringos" so here goes.

Communication is the **first** thing you must master. Do not practice your high-school or college Spanish in your business dealings. Most of the people you will deal with will probably speak English. If you want to practice your Spanish do it somewhere your income does not depend on it. And avoid Spanglish at all costs. If you invest in learning Spanish make sure to learn business and financial terms.

Secondly do not assume that Latinos, regardless of their country of origin, education, or level of business experience, are not as smart as you. Latinos are "street-smart" and that's what matters most.

Third, drop (as quickly as possible) the sales talk and avoid (completely) the bullshit. You may think that you need to "warm them up" with small talk. Most Latinos can socialize forever but when it comes time to do business — it's time to do business.

Fourth think relationship rather than transaction. Latinos are all about relationships — trust and integrity matter.

Doing business in the United States and doing business in Latin America are two different worlds. Doing business in the United States is fast-paced and is often done by the seat-of-the-pants. Rules are sometimes made up on the spot and there is little value given to commitments. Commitments are quickly and easily made — and often quickly and easily broken and forgotten.

Depending on their origin and experiences many Latinos do not trust banks and other financial institutions because, in some countries, a bank "holiday" means that the government has ordered the bank to remain closed until it can be audited and declared solvent.

Perhaps the most important thing when doing business with Latinos in the United States or in Latin America is to quickly establish trust — and to maintain that trust.

To a very large extent being a Latino is like being a member of a very large exclusive club where there are no formal applications or membership requirements.

One interesting aspect is that, outside of gang conflicts, there is no "bad blood" between Latinos of different national origins. Wars between countries are now centuries old, because most Latinos share (basically) the same language and (mostly) the same religion, there are not many real conflicts (with the distinct exception of fútbol). Compare this to Asians where there's hostile feelings between countries.

In many ways being Latino is like being a member of a very large family. Maybe it's like being a "made man" — a fully initiated member of the **Mafia**.

Being Latino or successfully doing business with Latinos means so much more than fluently speaking Spanish or knowing the difference between a cheap and ultra-premium Tequila.

More important than learning Spanish is learning about Latino Culture — how to live "la vida loca". Immerse yourself in Latino music, food, people, and geography.

And *try* to understand how Latinos **feel** about Gringos. And that's going to be your biggest challenge because there is no one stereotypical answer. It's like trying to understand how someone feels about ice cream and what's their favorite flavor. Most Gringos have no clue about Latinos. But here's what one Latina has to say about Gringos:

And gringos love Mexican food.

— Selena (Jennifer Lopez)
Selena (1997)

It's not whom you know.
It's not how much money you have.
It's whether or not you have the edge
and have the guts to use it.

— Mark Cuban

RHYTHM IS GONNA GET YOU
ROBERT MILLER

Let me tell you something. There is no nobility in poverty. I've been a rich man, and I've been a poor man. And I choose rich every fucking time. Cause, at least when I have to face my problems, I show up in the back of a limo wearing a $2,000 suit … and $40,000 gold fuckin' watch!

— Jordan Belfort (Leonardo DiCaprio)
The Wolf of Wall Street (2013)

Maybe you don't want to know the cold, hard truth about money. Maybe you have a fear of being rich — super rich! In *The Wolf of Wall Street* Jordan Belfort says: "The only thing standing between you and your goal is the bullshit story you keep telling yourself as to why you can't achieve it.

Jordan Belfort is right on! There is no nobility in poverty. So, dare to be rich. What do you think about this *propuesto indecente* from Leonardo DiCaprio in *The Wolf of Wall Street:*

"Now, if anyone here thinks I'm superficial or materialistic. Go get a job at fucking McDonald's because that's where you fucking belong. But, before you depart this room full of winners, I want you to take a good look at the person next to you, go on. Because sometime in the not-so-distant future, you're pullin' up to a red light in your beat-up old fucking Pinto and that person's gonna pull up right along side of you in a brand new Porsche, with their beautiful wife by his side who's got big voluptuous tits. And who will you be next to? Some disgusting wildebeest with three days of razon-stubble in a sleeveless muumuu, crammed in next to you with a carload full of groceries from the fucking Price Club! That's who you're gonna be sitting next to."

Although this "motivational speech" might cross the lines of good taste and definitely is politically incorrect in many ways, it's message is much deeper than the choice between a Pinto and a Porsche — it's about daring to be rich.

RHYTHM IS GONNA GET YOU

At some point in your life, if it hasn't already happened, the *rhythm is gonna get you.* What do I mean by that? You are going to realize what's really important in your life and discover how you can make it happen.

It's not about working hard — it's really all about doing everything you can to keep from working hard.

But you must want to realize your dreams more than you want anything. Imagine being in the ocean and drowning. As your lungs fill with water all you want is to breathe. You must want to make your dreams come true as much as you want to breathe.

Finally, life is all about creating your own rhythm — making your own music. Hold on tight to your dreams — all of them. Reach for the stars — all of them. Color outside the lines — and erase as many of them as you can. Make your own music and sing your own songs. Dance on the edge. Dare to be great. Love and allow yourself to be loved. And wash your hands for lunch.

Only those who will risk going too far can possibly find out how far one can go.

— T.S. Eliot

ABOUT US

All writers are vain, selfish and lazy, and at
the very bottom of their motives lies a
mystery. Writing a book is a long,
exhausting struggle, like a long bout of
some painful illness. One would never
undertake such a thing if one were not
driven by some demon whom one can
neither resist or understand.

— George Orwell

**This is the third book which we have written
together and we are excited to share our ideas
We are available to personally help you.**

**RobertMiller@RobertMiller.com
RobertMiller.com**

**Henry@HenryParksRoadtoAMillion
HenryParksRoadtoAMillion.com**

ROBERT MILLER

A native tenth generation Californian with Latino roots, I grew up fascinated with the Latino Culture

The last real Latina in my family was my great-grandmother who made my baby clothes and made me unlimited *tortillas de harina* that she patted out on a cloth flour bag that was turned inside out. I remember that and the red Cudahy box of lard that made the tortillas so delicious — but makes me cringe as a long-time vegan. The lard was a necessary ingredient of our tortillas, frijoles, tamales and only God knows what else!

When I was in kindergarten I made a school project that was a topographical map of Latin America on a giant sheet of plywood. Over the years I have travelled to all of the countries on my map and met my wife, Ali, in Bogotá, Colombia (my favorite country).

I been advising individuals, businesses, and governments for over five decades

HENRY PARK

Growing uo in Hawaiian Gardens, California — a city that was then and still remains predominately Latino — the Latino community was a very big part of my childhood. And being Korean made me a definite minority. Ironically, the Latino kids thought I was rich because I was Asian but the numbers did not add up for me. My parents both worked hard, and we constantly struggled financially.

You can read more about my story at KeepingUpWiththeParks.com and on my family's Facebook Group Keeping Up With the Parks.

Latinos play an enormous role in almost all aspects of my business and for that reason I joined Robert in writing what we hope will be a life-changing book for you.

Please visit my Facebook Group Henry Park's Road to A Million and join my weekly Zoom meetings every Friday at 5:00 PM (CA time). Meeting ID: 589-380-4727.

If, for some reason, you still don't understand what a Latino is, we challenge you to listen to the following song (YouTube Music) by Orchestra de la Luz — a Japanese salsa band formed in 1984:

SALSA CALIENTE DE JAPON

MÚSICA

Here are a few of our favorite songs presented in no particular order. Send us an email and let us know your favorite Latino songs.
RobertMillerNow@Gmail.com

Light My Fire — José Feliciano
Alicia Adorada — Carlos Vives
Amparo Arrebato — Richie Ray & Bobby Cruz
Copacabana — Barry Manilow
Buenos Aires — Madonna
Me and Julio Down by the Schoolyard
—Paul Simon
Richie's Jala Jala — Richie Ray & Bobby Cruz
The Tijuana Jail — Kingston Trio
La Bamba — Richie Valens
Sonida Bestial — Richie Ray & Bobby Cruz
Oye Como Va
— (Santana | Celia Cruz | Tito Puente)
Carnival — Celia Cruz
Vivir Mi Vida — Marc Anthony

MÚSICA

Livin' la Vida Loca — Ricky Martin
Hips Don't Lie — Shakira
Ay Jalisco No Te Rajes — Jorge Negrete
Will U Still Love Me Tomorrow
— Leslie Grace
Be My Baby — Leslie Grace
La Bomba — Azul Azul
Rhythm Is Gonna Get You — Gloria Estefan
Hawái —Maluma
Despacito — Luis Fonsi and Daddy Yankee
Mi Gente — J. Balvin and Willy William
Bailando —Enrique Iglesias
Gracias Amor — Matecaña Orchesta
Sensualidad
— Bad Bunny, Prince Royce and J. Balvin
Tijuana Taxi — Herb Alpert
Loco — Enrique Inglesias
Gente de Zona
— La Gozandera and Marc Anthony
El Cantante — Héctor Levoe
El Todopoderosa — Héctor Levoe
Montuno Street — Azabache
Bidi Bidi Bom Bom — Selena

MY PLAYLIST

JOSE FELICIANO

José Feliciano was the first Latin Artist to successfully cross over to the English music market and led the way for today's Latino superstars.

He was born blind to humble beginnings and had a signature style with his signature acoustic guitar and slow tempo.

In 1968 Feliciano released a cover version of the Door's song *Light My Fire* in a Latin style and in 1978 released his *Feliz Navidad* album — the title song is recognized as one of the top 25 all-time Christmas songs played around the world.

Feliciano is a 9-time Grammy award winner and performed alongside Bob Dylan, Frank Sinatra, Jimi Hendrix, and Johnny Cash.

The Night I Stopped Dating Blondes and Started Dating Latinas
By Robert Miller

It was one of those magical summer nights in Orange County — Friday, September 3, 1965 to be exact. I had graduated from high school in June and was in college and working nights at Douglas Aircraft in Long Beach. But that night I was invited to the Golden Bear in Huntington Beach to meet and listen to José Feliciano —a Puerto Rican who's career was on fire.

My date was a Huntington Beach "surfer girl" — right out of the Beach Boys song of the same name. She was a "model" who appeared on *The Dating Game* three months after our date.

A surfer from Seal Beach, I was a local at the Golden Bear and always got the VIP treatment with upfront seating. So when I arrived with my date (let's call her Dorothy) We were seated right next to the stage.

UNA HISTORIA

We met José and it's important to note that
he was sitting on stage wearing sunglasses
and accompanied by his guide dog.

Feliciano performed *La Bamba* — a
Meexican folk song which had been a Top
40 Hit in 1958 (the year before he died in
an airplane crash with Buddy Holly and J.P.
"the Big Bopper" Richardson).

Right after Feliciano finished *La Bamba*
Dorothy whispered into my ear the words I
will never forget: "Robert, is he blind?"
Before I answered, I repeated the words to
myself: "Robert, is he blind?"

For probably the first time in my then 18
years I was speechless. But I soon
recovered and, not wanting anyone to hear,
wrote these words on a cocktail napkin:
"Yes, he is blind. He was born blind, That's
why he is wearing sunglasses in here at
night. And, that's his guide dog next to him.
Feliciano was living in Los Angeles and saw
him a few months later and laughed and
asked: "Es una rubia?' And that's when I
stopped dating blondes.

C19 ECONOMICS

YOUR GUIDE TO PERSONAL AND BUSINESS FINANCE

ROBERT
MILLER

HENRY
PARK

ROBERT MILLER
HENRY PARK

FADING DREAMS
AND
RISING FEARS
AMERICA ON THE EDGE

THE MAGIC
OF
SELLING

ROBERT MILLER

RAINMAKING

ROBERT MILLER

SECOND WIND

THE MAGIC OF MAKING YOUR LIFE GREAT AGAIN

ROBERT MILLER

HENRY PARK'S

ROAD TO A
MILLION

HENRY PARK

HENRY PARK'S
ROAD TO A MILLION

COLLECTOR'S EDITION

HENRY PARK